Spiritual Laws

That Govern Humanity
and the
Universe

▽　　▽　　▽

D1502461

Spiritual Laws
That Govern Humanity and the Universe

by

Lonnie C. Edwards, M.D.

AMORC

Published by the Grand Lodge of the
English Language Jurisdiction, AMORC, Inc.
1342 Naglee Avenue, San Jose, CA 95191
www.rosicrucian.org

ISBN 1-893971-10-4

Library of Congress Control Number: 2005930132

10 9 8 7 6 5 4 3 2 1

Printed and bound in U.S.A.

Front Cover photo by Michal Eben, F.R.C., Grand Master,
Grand Lodge of the Czech and Slovakian Languages Jurisdiction, AMORC

Printed on 100% post-consumer fiber
using soy-based ink.

Acknowledgment and Dedication

I would like to gratefully acknowledge the support of Grand Master Julie Scott, who conceived the idea of these essays. Her enthusiasm and encouragement made this publication possible.

I would also like to express my appreciation for the inspiration, light, and love received through our Imperator, Christian Bernard, and the Rosicrucian Order, AMORC.

I acknowledge the indispensable, untiring, dedicated, and demanding assistance of my daughter, Lonnette Edwards, in preparing this work for publication.

These essays are dedicated to God, that Supreme Being who is within each reader and person and whose Spirit flows through each printed word of these essays. May they serve to inspire, bless, enlighten, and heal all of humanity.

Lonnie C. Edwards, M.D.

February 2005
Chicago, Illinois

Table of Contents

" . . . you have experienced

various cultures, races, creeds,

and beliefs on your path to evolution.

Respect all of these,

for they are a part of you . . . "

CHAPTER 1

Commitment to the Soul

*T*he true mystical spirit, as practiced by us, needs to be rededicated, strengthened, revived, and renewed. At no other time in human history have the souls of humanity had a greater need for expressing themselves through personality. Likewise, no better time has existed before now for humanity, individually and collectively, to honor and commit itself to the prompting and integrity of the indwelling soul.

The intelligent qualities of soul and soul personality must be given the freedom to express themselves through human activities without obstruction. Preparations must be made before the soul can express itself through this medium. We must desire that all obstacles interfering with the soul's expression of love and oneness of being be eliminated and replaced with light. The personality must be regenerated, enlightened, disciplined, purified, and dedicated to the service of humanity and to the glory of God.

From a practical point of view, we must strive to become aware of all negative, destructive, or unkind thoughts, feelings, beliefs, or intentions which might serve to block the flow of light coming from soul and soul personality. A sense of fulfillment, joy, and security develop by encouraging the soul to express its attributes through one's personality. Desire and ambition of a selfish nature diminish. There is no desire for power over any person, place, or condition. Instead, the soul begins to instill a sense of harmlessness. A commitment to express the higher self brings about much less criticism of others. Attacks upon our brethren, especially in instances when they seem to have fallen from the path, made a mistake, or expressed an opinion that differs sharply from our own, all fade into insignificance. Expressing the attributes of the soul develops a desire to have Divine Love flow continuously through and from the heart during inter-personal relationships. As this love flows, it communicates the desire to be the sole energy that exits from our mind and heart.

One of the purposes of universal soul, that special extension of God that is within, is to evolve the soul personality. The soul personality is to move toward master-ship and express God's attributes with increasing perfection. Before entering the earth plane and while in the cosmic realm, the soul personality desires, understands, and accepts this reality. It neither thinks nor functions as the human mind, nor does it have the traditional fears, limited under-standing, and reservations of the human personality.

The soul personality, guided by God's will and wisdom, desires and decides exactly what experiences it needs in order to accomplish its divine mission: a divine unity with

God. In achieving this, it becomes, just as the Creator is, kind, loving, forgiving, and patient. The soul personality and God are inseparable during this earthly human journey and are always available to guide and infuse you with unconditional love and understanding in all endeavors.

The soul encourages you to be proactive in all experiences; being reactive is destructive. Contact and unity with the soul bring understanding and answers your questions. God has so designed us that within each of us there is a special classroom, an inner sanctum, designed for inner communion. Within this classroom, your master teacher expects and awaits you. Seek the presence of this Master Within. No one can enter this classroom except you. The Master is always there.

When the soul personality leaves the cosmic realm with the lessons to be learned, it makes the commitment to carry out its mission here on the earth plane while retaining the wisdom acquired during previous incarnations. With the first breath of life, the soul personality enters the body and finds that it is imprisoned in this physical entity with underdeveloped senses and a minimal awareness. A newborn infant is not equipped to communicate or connect with the physical world in a very intelligible fashion. However, this physical world, with its experiences and human contacts, is absolutely essential to the work that the soul agreed to for the purpose of evolving and expressing godlike qualities.

The soul personality, responding to God's laws and directions, continues the process of creating the important physical instruments through which it will work and develop. These include the five physical senses; the endocrine and psychic centers; and the central, sympathetic, and spinal nervous systems. All of these are active and gradually grow and further develop. Among the physical body's most notable component is the brain, along with its attributes of intellect, desires, and emotions. A wonderful and efficient physical instrument results: a perfect temple in which the soul will dwell.

The soul personality devotes so much attention, energy, and effort in developing the physical body and its faculties that the soul personality forgets its true identity and its mission or purpose. It begins to identify with the body as "self." Under the light of God, it begins to understand its true nature and self. It comes to understand that the physical body with all its wonderful attributes does not constitute the real self. The journey back home begins, the journey to express its godlike qualities.

Let us briefly consider the mind. Mind is a part of universal mind. We might conclude that one of the functions of mind is to transmit the will and desires of the soul to the brain. The mind is truly the great "sixth" sense, designed to serve as a special instrument for the soul. The student of mysticism needs to meditate on the concepts dealing with the reality of the physical body and its relationship to the soul, the soul's mission and purpose. Understanding and being conscious of this permits us to commit our lives toward God's purpose.

The indwelling soul is love, light, and love, and operates according to the cosmic law of love. We seek to establish this identity and we desire to express the soul's attributes through our human personality. We manifest light, love, and peace the more we strive to be tolerant, kind, loving, idealistic, and selfless. This attitude establishes a harmonious attunement and relationship with creative cosmic forces. The soul will begin to increasingly reveal itself in our daily lives.

What can we do to create, build, and express these qualities in our lives *now*? We must begin the process regardless of difficult relationships, problems, and associations we may have now or that we may expect in the future. Through study, contemplation, prayer, and desire we can commit ourselves to developing and expressing a loving heart and mind while showing greater generosity. We must be determined to increase our willingness to forgive, to overlook weakness and errors. We must be willing to extend a hand to those who seem to fall. We need to grasp every opportunity to maintain an inclusive mind. We must practice being open and broad-minded, tolerant and patient. We must learn to accept and love all life forms, including those that sacrifice themselves for our food, comfort, and emotional enjoyment. We must refuse to permit our consciousness to be tied solely to visible, earthly, negative, or bigoted thoughts of any kind, especially regarding creed, culture, or nationality.

Begin to realize that during the many incarnations through which you have lived, you have experienced various cultures, races, creeds, and beliefs on your path to evolution. Respect all of these, for they are a part of you or will be in the future. In this life you are given the opportunity to live and practice whatever you learned in past lives and experiences. In accordance with cosmic law, if you fail to do this, your "lesson plan" must be revised. Experiences must be repeated until they are learned and practiced. Consult the soul within and let it guide and walk the path with you.

Provide yourself with quiet time to go into your inner sanctum. Attune with the Master Within. One way of doing this is to begin before you even sit down by becoming quiet and mentally stating, "I intend to commune with God and my soul." Or you may choose to say, "I intend to commune with my higher mind." Then sit down comfortably, becoming still, while breathing slowly and deeply, relaxing and focusing upon the movement of your breath. State your intention as many times as necessary for sincerity of heart and mind to get started and take control. When this happens, you will feel a sacred bonding emotion and a relaxing feeling. As you repeat this daily ritual, you will gradually begin to sense a great spiritual peace in heart and mind. Awareness of this appeal and subsequent success may be realized consciously or unconsciously. Even when you think you have felt nothing, you have still achieved an important degree of success.

The great law of love gradually becomes the law of your being and the intention of your life. Recognize love and beauty as the sole essences of all existence, the most dynamic and healing forces in the universe. Learn to see and sense these all around you on your path. Actively choose to have this love govern how you deal with people, places, and conditions. Engender a true soul commitment and experience true inner peace. Fear and resentment cannot exist where this law rules. You are truly dedicated to soul's purpose whenever operating within this cosmic and universal law. You may experience the same infusion of spirit which inspired St. Francis of Assisi to write the following while in contact with the Infinite:

Make me an instrument of Thy Peace.
Where there is hate, let me bring love.
Where there is offense, let me bring forgiveness.
Where there is discord, let me bring union.
Where there is error, let me bring truth.
Where there is doubt, let me bring faith.
Where there is despair, let me bring hope.
Where there is darkness, let me bring light.

Where there is sadness, let me bring joy.
O Lord, I do not seek so much to be consoled as to console,
To be understood as to understand,
To be loved as to love.
For it is in giving that we receive,
It is in forgetting ourselves that we find ourselves,
It is in forgiving that we are forgiven,
It is in dying that we are reborn to eternal life.

Forever realize that you are a source of God's light and love. So Mote It Be!

Let's Apply What We've Learned . . .

Exercise to Strengthen Commitment to the Soul

Sit comfortably in your chair with feet flat on the floor and hands in your lap. Slowly and gently take seven deep breaths. Pause for a count of four after each inhalation, then open your mouth and slowly exhale. Closing your eyes, contemplate the nature of the soul in light of the chapter you have just read. Then open your eyes and read aloud the following five affirmations. After reading each affirmation, pause briefly in order to contemplate the essential meaning and seek to experience each of the affirmations as a true reality.

1. Yes, I am a living soul.
2. I am forever enfolded within the very soul of God.
3. My body is a perfect instrument of my indwelling soul.
4. Yes, I dwell within this wonderful, magnificent body for which I am grateful.
5. I intend for soul to express its light and love through me to all with whom I come in contact and who are in my world.

After finishing your contemplation, offer thankfulness. You may say any prayer you wish and send thoughts of cosmic love and cosmic light to those in the world and to those with whom you are in contact. Afterwards take five deliberate breaths, and then write in your journal any impressions of meaning of the soul that you care to record. Go about your regular activities after finishing this exercise.

"Life . . . . is a creative work

for which we are

the artist, architect,

engineer, and builder."

CHAPTER 2

The Continuum of Life
and the World of Relationships

*L*ife expresses itself as one grand and glorious continuum. Life begins, protected in the healthy womb, and then flows from infancy through childhood, adolescence, adulthood, and on into our mature years. Each of these stages of life is intimately connected to the previous stage. Because of this interconnection, each stage of life receives and exerts a powerful influence upon those stages preceding it and those following it.

To truly understand this concept and make practical use of its value for teaching us a better way of fulfilling our lives, we must first enlarge our understanding of who we really are. What is the essential purpose of our lives? What is the meaning we are meant to contribute to the wholeness of life? As we ask ourselves these questions, we must stop thinking of our purpose and our meaning as being singular and confined to the short span in which we will live on this earth. We must begin, instead, to think of our lives and our contributions as a part of that great and glorious continuum that we share in space and time. Our oneness in this chain of events, of which we are a part and to which we will make our contribution, refines and evolves the continuum on this plane for centuries to come.

As I look into the face of a newborn infant, I see a micro-image and a reflection of that continuum. In my mind's eye I see that infant striving to become a living part of the fabric of society. Even before this, I see the unborn child making preparation for the coming newborn infant as the physical body develops into its various systems: endocrine, cardiovascular, reproductive, and so forth.

I see the spiritual body of the infant striving toward "becoming"—seeking its nourishment of love, soothing rhythmic sounds, and harmonic feelings. I see "mind" drawing on all of these as it pushes forth toward its best potential. I see the precious infant drawing at the same time upon its inborn potential and its external environment. Along the continuum we are called to help this micro-reflection of ourselves—and our greater collective selves—to release its full potential. The wholeness of life is in our hands, and we are a part of that wholeness.

As this precious infant's life is reborn into the earthly environment, I also see that it is born into a "world of relationships." The characteristics, meaning, and purpose of these relationships vary with regard to character, quality, and quantity. They may be pleasurable, challenging, stimulating, rewarding, spiritual, loving, or of many more types. All of these relationships are designed to aid the infant in its growth and evolvement, and they provide an opportunity for it to add to the glorious continuum of life. The infant's travels and experiences are a micro-image of our own.

Relationships characterize our earthly lives. The manner and attitude in which we deal with these relationships determine their overall outcome, as well as the effect they will have upon our sense of physical, mental, emotional, psychological, and spiritual well-being.

All relationships provide an opportunity for the Divine to flow to and through us. When the Creative Divine flows from us, it connects with its kind in others, and the resulting contact produces greater light. When our consciousness observes this, a feeling or sense of being separate is lost. The realization comes that we are experiencing the "one life" secretly veiled in many bodies. Our challenge is to see and live beyond the appearance of the veil.

This world of relationships provides the opportunity for us to participate constructively in the glorious continuum of life and the unfolding of Divine Universal Intelligence in all human affairs. These relationships include human beings and all life forms. They are at all levels and in all activities of organizations, groups, individuals, families, friends, tribes, and clans. All these varieties of relationships provide the same opportunities if we but face them with a broader vision of unity, seeing ourselves in those with whom and for whom we interact. Seeing beyond and through the illusory veils that separate us is necessary. In addition, always realizing the God Within, we can see the face of God in those with whom we relate.

We can innately be the Divine and permit the Divine to flow through us to others. Intuitively, when we think of the Divine, thoughts of light, love, beauty, patience, understanding, and compassion bathe our mind and consciousness. When we assume the attitude of Divinity, our relationships become meaningful and we perceive and accomplish the cosmic lessons they bring. This is the means by which the grand and glorious continuum of life evolves and contributes to all humanity.

In the world of relationships we must make choices. As we function in this world, we discover that there are alternatives for the actions, thoughts, motives, or beliefs facing us. To make wise choices, we need to always bear in mind the resources that are ours to use. Prudent thinking and the capacity to scrutinize thinking are part of those resources. Our will and emotions must be poised and balanced. We must bring into consciousness some degree of foresight and futurity, for these will permit us to consider the consequences.

The recognition of choices is extremely important to the student seeking growth and spirituality. The art of being aware of choices and then exercising and demonstrating wisdom in selection must be acquired. In the process of learning to make wise choices, many spiritual attributes are developed. As human beings we recognize that free will is an inherent human attribute and right. We must also realize that as human beings we must accept and live with our choices and our preferences, be they good or "bad." The student should regard this as a right as well as a divine endowment.

We are taught that we must walk through the pillars of opposites. This means that we must also wrestle with pairs of opposites. In so doing, we learn to acquiesce in favor of a greater principle over a lesser one. Here is where we learn to distinguish between "good," "better," and "'best," and to realize that the good of the whole transcends self-interest and the ego. Here is where the sincere student begins to exercise the will freely and gradually use its tremendous and enormous power for spiritual purposes— for right action and right relationship. We must become increasingly aware that life with its myriad experiences is not something that happens to us unbidden; it is a creative work for which we are the artist, architect, engineer, and builder. By experiencing chaos, we sometimes learn how to make life's best choices. Questions will appear to be more simple, and yet of utmost importance. For as the student is drawn to seek the Master Within, and hence is drawn closer to his or her soul, this influence will make the line of choice become clear and well defined. So Mote It Be!

Let's Apply What We've Learned . . .

Exercise for Contemplating the Continuum of Life

(Read silently or aloud three times before performing.)

Sit in contemplation for a few moments regarding the continuum of life and how you have been a part of this great continuum. Then visualize your participation in your present life.

"Life gradually ceases

to be without design,

and its experiences cease

to be meaningless

or ill planned."

CHAPTER 3

Creating and Maintaining Spiritual Stamina

*O*ur true self is created in the image of God, the Supreme Being, the Supreme Creator. This has been repeated and written many times. Either consciously or unconsciously, we begin to search for that image and likeness of which we are created. Through that search, we acquire a desire to know who we truly are—to discover the real self.

That longing to know, and that eternal search, has led us to a consciousness of adoration, worship, praise, thankfulness, service, and prayer. The very nature of our soul begins to infuse and pour through our feelings, thoughts, and words. These can be heard humbly, sincerely, and silently uttering praise and adoration:

> *God of our Heart, God of our Realization, Thou who art Creator of all life, visible and invisible, manifest and unmanifest, Maker of all stars, planets, and worlds, Father-Mother of every soul; Thou, God, the All-Powerful, the All-Knowing, the Ever-Present Being, whose dwelling place is everywhere, even in the hearts of humankind—individually and collectively, we would talk to Thee and worship Thee this hour.*

Attune and harmonize our souls with Thee, with the intention that our physical bodies may become and continue to be a perfect temple in which to dwell, a segment and extension of Thyself.

God, we recognize and believe all healing— physical, mental, and spiritual—to be divine. The good that we have done and do is because Thou hast blessed our efforts, rewarded our faith and the faith of those whom we have served. God, help us to realize that every person is a soul, even as ourselves. By the mystic Law of Assumption, let us be our brother and our sister that we may better know his or her needs and once knowing these, supply.

To all acquired and available knowledge, may there be added the Divine Gift of Intuition, in order that errors in judgment and diagnoses may grow less and less. Through disharmony or loss of perfect attunement with Thee, we may fail temporally to interpret and understand our brother or sister's needs or give them the wrong advice. At such times, may it please Thee, God, to speak to and through our brother and sister to the end that they will be guided not to choose or accept what we may have in error advised.

God, help us to realize that when we have administered unto and treated the material or physical concerns and needs of our brothers and sisters, we have only half-finished our task.

Thou hast taught us that human beings are dual beings; we are physical and we are also spiritual. Knowing this, help us to be your servants, helpers unto this spiritual self. We have come to know that we can only serve Thee as we serve humanity; we can only love Thee as we love our brothers and sisters. For Thou art one with all of humanity and Thou art our brothers and sisters.

Serving humankind, always, on every plane—the physical, the mental, the emotional, the psychological and the spiritual—we would become like unto the Great Physician, even Christ.

So Mote It Be!

With such total sincerity and commitment uttering from the heart, spiritual stamina is born. With constant and daily reflection upon what is sounded forth in this petition, spiritual stamina will be maintained. Veiled within the petition is the message that we can, with the proper utilization of our faculties, come to know the various attributes and possibilities of the spiritual world, our divine soul, and of the Infinite.

We draw cosmic light, understanding, and love to us as we, properly and with the purpose of service, use the attributes of imagination, imaging, visualization, perceiving, and feeling. These qualities are then reflected throughout our true nature. The soul and spiritual self will radiate divine light through us, revealing attributes of their nature, as we use these attributes in service to ourselves and to others.

Attributes of the soul and spiritual self teach and guide us in our journey through both the material and immaterial worlds. A commitment to utilize and manifest our understanding of the teachings that come to us develops our spiritual stamina. During periods of contemplation and silence, information comes to us either consciously or subconsciously which we endeavor to manifest as our understanding of life evolves. Life gradually ceases to be without design, and its experiences cease to be meaningless or ill-planned.

An important key to remember is that we are, creatively, to utilize and condition our physical or material experiences so that they can transmit and express what lies behind and above their nature. The inner faculties of our being are innately designed to receive and transmit those divine and spiritual energies in which we live, move, and have our being.

Exercises intended to develop our psychic abilities appear in our mystical teachings. It is important to know, however, that these exercises and experiments do not complete the evolutionary purpose for psychic development. We must learn and practice the ability to absorb, transmit, and reflect the higher spiritual energies through the psychic faculties. These faculties then become instruments for soul purposes. (The student is cautioned and warned not to use these faculties to transmit or reflect for selfish and destructive purposes.)

Spiritual stamina is developed as our higher spiritual energies flow through the psychic nature and, by means of service, stamina is maintained. These must flow with love for all of life. The spiritualized psychic faculties become instruments for delivering God's blessings and cosmic service.

To be whole and free is to live and manifest on the material and immaterial planes in harmony with the spiritual laws that govern all that there is. It then becomes our duty and responsibility to transmit and reflect in our daily lives, and to our utmost ability, the highest vibrations of the universe and of our Creator.

So Mote It Be!

"Universal truth

recognizes

the oneness of life

and the

oneness of being."

CHAPTER 4

Creating Peace and Unconditional Love

I can hear the cries of the trees and the forest as they, with a gentle power, unfold and struggle to proclaim their right to make a contribution to the harmony, health, beauty, and peace of the planet. They struggle to proclaim this in the only way that they can. I hear the unity of the birds as they send their ethereal sounds, harmonizing the air. I watch the instinctive movements and sounds of all the animals that walk and crawl on the face of the earth as they try their best to harmonize and respond to the laws of nature. I can see and hear the rhythmic motion and intelligent communications of all the life forms that swim the waters of the planet proclaiming the majesty and beauty of their Creator. All of these forms, infused with life and purpose, are expressing a magnificent spirit, power, and force: the URGE TO BE.

Clearly and distinctly, I also hear the many voices of humankind desperately struggling to communicate their perception of individuality and purpose through their many languages, nations, ethnicities, races, and religious groups. All of these expressing a profound power and spirit: the Urge to be. The voices of humankind can be heard crying their prayers for love, protection, security, guidance, and right action. I can also hear humankind's voices of greed and selfishness. The language of one group of beings is poorly understood, if at all, by the other groups.

I understand that all of these cries and pleas originate from the same source and all express the same urge. That source is the very essence of Life itself—a divine attribute of God, of Supreme Being. This divine attribute of God announces and proclaims Its intention and Its will. That universal will and spirit manifest through all of life as an URGE TO BE.

We who claim to have been given dominion over all the earth and all life forms therein must realize that the true essence of life proclaims and announces the oneness of Being and the interdependence of all of life. A sense of intelligence and knowledge of the oneness of life lies within our being, ready to provide the ability and wisdom to see and hear with the eyes and ears of the soul. This attunement manifests as goodwill and right action toward all life.

We are often asked to comment on what is happening in the world today. What about the conditions and happenings in the Middle East, in Europe, in Africa, Iraq, Asia, America, and China? All of these questions are seeking to understand with some depth the state of human consciousness in various areas on the planet. They are seeking an understanding and purpose of human events.

They seek to understand the evolution of humankind and human consciousness, thought, and purpose.

Every day, every hour, and every minute millions of people throughout the world are praying for peace and searching for empowerment. Within their hearts burns a desire to attain the kind of life that would provide them with freedom from fear and uncertainty. The extent of their prayers for peace is dependent upon the concept, measure, and function of the world in which they live. The depth and feeling of their prayers are generated to a large extent by the discomfort touching their daily lives.

Some of these people desire an inner peace—a peace of mind, which is limited to their own world of self. They feel that this can be attained with little or no concern for their fellow humans. Others pray for an ethnic or religious peace—to be empowered ethnically, racially, or religiously. They desire a change in position for their particular group— a redirection of fear, hate, and distrust. Their desire is to change only those conditions affecting a particular ethnic or religious group. They pray for a "just revenge." Among such individuals there is the belief that it is possible to have peace within one particular ethnic or religious group, without having deep concern for the welfare of all people, regardless of their ethnic, religious, or national origin. Such people live and think in a world that has been narrowed by humanity's ignorance, as well as by feelings of separateness that produce "classifications" within the human race.

There is still another group whose prayers for peace and power are directed toward a particular nation, with little thought for the contentment of other nations. There is an unspoken belief that it is not essential or important for all nations to have peace in order that their particular nation might enjoy it. They pray for the troubled mind of a national leader without including the desire for divine guidance for the leaders of nations throughout the world. As we become conscious of these prayers we cannot help but petition and desire that they become extended: that the little worlds be extended in scope and concern; that individuals not only desire peace for themselves, but for all fellow humans. Just as the desire for ethnic or religious peace becomes a desire for harmony among all groups, the desire for national peace must become a desire for international harmony.

The higher aspects of our being have the capacity to bring understanding, guiding and directing us in our roles as servants of humanity and co-creators of our environment. Universal truth recognizes the oneness of life and the oneness of being. One might say that there should be a sense of oneness in the "body of humanity." Great leaders and masters throughout the ages have taught this. If part of our body becomes diseased, the body responds in an attempt to heal the diseased part for the benefit of the whole body.

Our higher consciousness is able to understand and realize that whatever is happening in any part of the world, is happening within the body of humankind, within the body of all of life. Only our spiritual mind and being can see and acknowledge this.

We must rise to the higher aspect of our being, the aspect that has the capacity to love unconditionally and to understand and practice the oneness of being and of life. Those among us who have the ability to realize and perceive this, also have the opportunity to manifest it: to act, think, and pray accordingly.

We must return to the center within, where divine will and purpose is known, the center where spiritual realization of the unit structure of unconditional love can be found, and where the unit structure of peace is understood. We must gather unto ourselves the responsibility of not only realizing but also demonstrating our divine inner potential. We have the capacity to spread love and peace through our contacts. Our thoughts and hearts must carry the causative agents of harmony, peace, and love. The love in our thoughts and mind is contagious. If we are to understand the nature and cause of many of the conditions existing in the world today and in our personal lives, we must seek greater understanding of the universal laws that govern humanity. With a deep desire, with reflection, meditation, and contemplation these laws will be opened as portals through which each of us may enter, comprehend, and feel the profound understanding they bring. They will also bring meaning and application.

Our thoughts, feelings, and beliefs are vibratory agents and are contagious. The love in our thoughts, feelings, and motives is infectious. As we desire to understand universal truths, we will receive inspiration and commitment to accept individual responsibility toward creating and maintaining harmony in our personal environment and other aspects of our communal, civic, national, and international life. We have the responsibility to permit our spiritual self to assist humankind in evolving an understanding of the true nature of unity, harmony, and peace. Our collective intention is to become points of light shining on the paths traveled by humanity. Our collective light will lead humanity to where a true knowledge of peace and harmony may be found, and demonstrate how it will be created and maintained. Cosmic light on the path leads humans to understand that peace and harmony begin with the individual. All expressions of peace—be they personal, ethnic, religious, national, or international—begin within the personal aspiration of the individual. From there it grows and manifests in all human behavior.

If we desire to have peace in our lives, our homes, and our cities, peace in our country and the world, we must begin this complex process by developing peace within ourselves, eliminating acts of "war" within our daily lives, within our minds and thoughts. Are we carrying on a "thought war" with someone or creating a condition in our minds, motives, feelings, or intentions? Are we mentally and emotionally planning an attack or an invasion on any person or in any of our relationships? If so, let us sit down at the virtual peace table within, and negotiate and pledge a more honorable solution that can manifest as good will and right relations. We can then declare a state of peace within ourselves and in our relationships.

Cosmic law states that thoughts and feelings of peace are creative and will vibrate and radiate into the minds and hearts of humankind. When we think and express our intelligence in such a way that it serves our fellow human beings, we are spreading peace and understanding. As we respect the opinions of others, even when those opinions differ from our own, we are preventing war and creating peace. Unconditional love finds a way to radiate from us.

When we respect the feelings, rights, and properties of others, we are eliminating and preventing war and laying the foundation for environmental harmony and peace among all humans. When we can demonstrate honor and respect for what another human being has honestly acquired, and we are able to rejoice in that person's happiness and self-fulfillment, we are effectively preventing war and creating unconditional love and a state of peace within the human race. It should be our intention to reject all thoughts that we or any other person, culture, race, or kin are special and privileged, for we know that the Cosmic sees all people as special and privileged, because we are all children of the universe—all creations of the one Creator.

Our thoughts are contagious and they create and manifest their own kind—physically, emotionally, and spiritually. To create an environment of mutual respect, right relations, happiness, and harmony, we should have the intention in our hearts that all human beings have the right to advance in life, and that they have the right to think and live the way they choose, as long as they do not interfere with the rights, privileges, and dignity of others. This becomes our intention even though it might differ from the way we live and think.

When the divine qualities of the soul begin to flow through us, we will live as brothers and sisters. The intelligence of the soul expressing through us will demonstrate that success in life is not solely dependent upon power, fame, and riches; it is dependent on how well we express the potential of the indwelling soul. With this understanding and with practice, we can change our personal perceptions and the perceptions of those we contact. We can bring inner peace to our nature.

Universal laws decree that we permit love, compassion, and understanding to bathe our mind and the minds of humanity. To the degree that we think and act in harmony with this decree, inner wars will cease to exist within our mind and heart and also within the world of humanity. The higher self, the Divine Mind within each of us, must guide our thoughts, our reasoning, and our actions. We are destined to become creators of peace and harmony. We must strengthen our ability to love compassionately and unconditionally.

As our desires, beliefs, thoughts, and practices rise to such high qualities, God and the cosmic masters bless our efforts. Peace will prevail within the human mind and heart and on the earth. The intention for humanity is to proclaim the right of all men, women, and children of all nations, races, and ethnicities to believe in and worship the God of their choice. They also have the right to practice that belief in a harmonious environment.

Beloved, all of the above are the first steps to understanding the true nature of cosmic love and peace. These begin within us and spread throughout our personal and collective environment. We will utilize the total energies of our being—the inner and outer faculties—in creating and maintaining a paradise of peace and harmony. As written by many authors on the pages of wisdom in the Book of Life, "Think not that life is without design or ill planned. Life is the flowering of our thoughts—the very product of our hands."

Our intentions should always be to transmit the higher spiritual energies and meaning of life. All the great avatars, masters, and philosophers of the past and present have placed great emphasis upon the quality of our thoughts. They have demonstrated throughout their teachings how thought can and does modify our environment and experiences. Awareness of our thoughts must come first, followed by discipline of our routine thinking. We who are aware of the creative power of intentions, motives, thoughts, feelings, and beliefs have the opportunity to develop a sound and intelligent knowledge of how to practice habits and patterns of thought that are in harmony with the laws of nature and life. With practice, they can play an important role in bringing unconditional love, peace, happiness, and contentment into our lives and the lives of others. We will then truly understand in what manner:

> *Thought prays for us our prayers,*
> *Thought dispenses to us our realities,*
> *Thought limits for us that which is limited,*
> *Thought expands and extends for us that which is*
>   *expanded and extended,*
> *Thought heals and blesses.*

Indeed, the constructive, creative, and divine power of our thoughts creates for us our peace and grants unto us our true cosmic power. The inner spirit of every individual cries out, "Let there be peace, health, harmony, healing, love, and kindliness among all nations and people, and let these begin within my consciousness. Let them begin as my personal thoughts, beliefs, desires, and actions. My soul desires that I become a dispenser of peace for all humanity—for all of life." This is truly the origin of spiritual health and well-being.

As we find ourselves living more and more in a world where announcements of terror, strife, and confusion are common, we realize a true need for inner peace and imperturbability. We seek a state of being that is free from anxiety, fear, distrust, and insecurity. We know that disharmony of any type hinders our ability to function efficiently and effectively. When this state of mind appears, we know to take time out, breathe slowly and deeply in and out, becoming still and more relaxed with each breath.

We soon contact the indwelling presence that lies deep within, whose very nature is peace. We know that this divine presence has never left us and neither has its source of peace. This peace is always at the center of our being, willing and ready to flood our being and bring calmness. No matter whether the origin of any disturbance—world-related, news-related, or personal-related—we can let go of these and allow peace to enter and quietly infuse our consciousness. This peace has its origin within the soul and it stands ready to express itself in every experience and condition of our lives. Its action does not require and is not dependent upon the external world or conditions.

Let's Apply What We've Learned . . .
Exercise to Bring Peace

You always have the opportunity to choose peace. Take advantage of this right now as you read these words and engage in this inner experience.

Sit comfortably in your chair. Slowly, gently, and deeply take a few relaxing breaths. As you breathe in, quietly or silently say the word "God." As you exhale, quietly or silently say "God." Continue this breathing. The peace that you seek is from God and it will quiet any disturbance. This is peace as your soul knows it and each breath proclaims it. This peace surpasses all human understanding.

As you continue to relax and breathe and make the pronouncement, notice that all anxieties, fears, and worries are slowly disappearing as peace floods your entire being:

body, mind, and spirit. As you breathe, relax, and let go, the greater is your access to all the peace that you need. This peace is the very essence of your being. Your soul is dispensing this peace upon every atom, cell, and function of your mind and body. This condition and place of peace is always available to you. Know this and use it at any time. It is never separated from you as God is never separated from you. You need no longer feel afraid, alone, or disturbed. You are comforted, nurtured, serene, secure, and protected. The power of the Infinite is now flowing to and through you. Close your eyes and contemplate this peace for a few moments. Perform this exercise once a week for the next thirty days.

So Mote It Be!

"There is detachment from that

which is

transitory and illusory.

There is attachment to that which

is permanent,

eternal, and true."

CHAPTER 5

Detachment

*A*lthough the sincere student of mystical and spiritual life realizes that a state of detachment must be achieved if one is to advance toward mastership, this is usually the last development that the student seriously undertakes. This is perhaps postponed because human nature realizes that detachment requires a separation from all that is physically, emotionally, and psychologically possessed, and this is a difficult process that causes some suffering. Such possessions are true ties to selfishness and to that which is transient, ephemeral, illusory, and untrue.

If sincerely undertaken, a series of detachment processes will begin. Gradually and increasingly these processes develop into a major and important project. From the first steps upon the path, the student begins to undertake a certain amount of this process unknowingly and unconsciously. This happens when the soul is gradually awakened and seeks and desires its own identity. The soul no longer wishes to identify itself with the human personality, but seeks for the human personality to become identified with it. Thus begins the process that leads the human personality to lose its sense of separateness and its preoccupation with mundane qualities, the untrue and transient. The soul begins to encourage the human personality to assume a dispassionate perspective and a lack of concern for the possessions held by the emotional, physical, and psychological natures. True detachment encourages the soul to express its wisdom through the human personality.

In this manner the process of dispassion, followed by discrimination, and finally detachment, is begun. Consciously, this rhythm is slowly and progressively expressed through the personality. The objective analysis by the lower mind must not be allowed to define, interrupt, or color this soul process that is now making an impact upon the conscious personality.

Let us now turn our attention to the major inner process, which is evolving within our higher consciousness. This inner process occurs because of the intelligent energies of soul and the evolving soul personality. The effort, desire, and intention of the student should be to begin the process of placing the soul first in all the activities and affairs of his or her life and to become more devoted and attached to the purpose and will of the soul. This inner process begins to unfold as one of "attachment" to the soul. A lack of concern and a disinterest in many persons, things, places, and conditions that are not of a higher nature, begins to appear in the personality. Those mundane experiences and pleasures, which once brought much enjoyment to the outer self (the small human faculties and senses), are now perceived with increasing indifference and casualness. Inwardly these things are rejected, energy is withheld from them, and they are abandoned. Even so, there are no negative or destructive thoughts focused or directed toward them. A form of renunciation gradually and harmoniously takes place.

The beauty and power of the soul begins to shine through the evolving life. There is a favoring of all that enhances the higher self. The soul attracts minds and conditions that favor and act in harmony with the loving and creative laws of the universe. With the soul acting through the human personality, the personality begins to detach itself from all those possessions and attractions that were once given great importance and dominated one's life.

Through practices of contemplation, meditation, and inner silence, the student becomes aware of a profound inner process slowly and progressively externalizing into his or her life. The real inner and beautiful cosmic process that is taking place is part of an eternal unfolding of the rose of the soul personality. There is detachment from that which is transitory and illusory. There is attachment to that which is permanent, eternal, and true. The student begins to see his or her fellow humans as more beautiful souls evolving all the attributes of the Creator.

The student's intention now is to release and detach from any possessive hold on the material personal self. An effort to release and detach from his or her hold upon the personal selves of others also develops. It is now realized that such a hold is primarily for the human personality of others and of self, and only secondarily for the indwelling divine and eternal soul. In reality there is no loss when true soul attachment and/or detachment occurs, for the student's consciousness rises and expands upward and realizes that those who are loved, are now loved as souls. This love assumes a higher and eternal bond.

Detachment teaches the student how to truly serve others and humanity, without attachment to the results of that service. The need and expectation of praise disappears. In true service, the souls of all are united in communion and love. They are cognizant of, and render glory only to, the Supreme Creator of all that is in heaven and earth. In order for true detachment to bear fruition, it must begin within the soul. This will occur as the student seeks contact with the soul and makes a commitment to it.

So Mote It Be!

Let's Apply What We've Learned . . .

Exercise

(Read this exercise three times before performing.)

With eyes closed, sit comfortably in your seat with hands in your lap. Take seven deep breaths, breathing slowly in and slowly out. Sit still for a few moments, then take another deep breath and imagine that your consciousness is flowing with supreme gentleness up, up, and into the heavens, shining as a white light, brilliant and beautiful.

As it flows higher and higher, feel God's divine love surrounding and enfolding you. You soon realize that you have attuned with the mind of God. You feel safe, secure, and protected in this divine presence. Become still and silent and, with gentleness of mind, sense God's love and wisdom bathing your entire being—every cell of your body, mind, and spirit. Your soul personality is refreshed and joyful. Remain in this manner for a few seconds.

Afterwards take seven more deliberate, deep breaths, and begin your descent back to the earth plane. Take another deep breath. Feel yourself seated comfortably, and feel your feet upon the floor. Take another breath and, feeling refreshed and wide awake, open your eyes. Remain seated for a while before rising and going about your activities.

"The Rosicrucian Order's teachings

. . . reveal the knowledge

and ageless wisdom

that govern the universe."

CHAPTER 6

The Essence of the
Rosicrucian Order's Teachings

*A*s you begin reading this chapter, please sit comfortably in your seat. Breathe slowly in and out, center yourself inwardly, and realize that you are in the very presence of God. This realization and attunement will aid you in understanding the meaning of this message.

Continue to breathe slowly in and slowly out. Throughout this reading, realize that you are breathing God's sweet and holy air into your body. Recognize also that God is breathing for you and that God has given to you the gift of life. God has always loved you. Continue to breathe gently and deeply, slowly in and slowly out. God first breathed the breath of life into your body and has always been connected with you since that first breath at your birth. That first breath contained your living soul. You became an individualized living image of God housed within God's temple, your physical body. From that moment forward, God has dwelled within you, waiting for your awakening to his presence. This divine presence always abides, stirs, and functions within your being. As you read the following petition, feel the sincerity of its intentions.

O Divine Intelligence within my physical structure, grant unto me the privilege of attuning with Thee. Although I do not know Thee perfectly, of Thine existence I am sure. Calm my fiery and selfish anxiety to know Thee perfectly. Transmute this into gentle feelings and vibrations of enthusiasm, so that I may realize my closeness and oneness with Thee. Let my desire be only to love and serve Thee.

Tell my mortal consciousness again, and again and again, that I can only love Thee, as I love each human being; I can only serve Thee, as I serve my brothers and sisters. Let me truly understand that Thou art my fellow human beings and just as Thou art my brothers and sisters. Grant unto me the light to truly comprehend that we are all divine extensions of Thee. We are all truly divine extensions.

So Mote It Be!

Perhaps you have asked, "What is the goal of the various discourses and exercises given to the Rosicrucian student? What does the Rosicrucian Order seek to accomplish?" A complete answer is not possible in the form and manner that is usually expected. The goal of the Order is not to change the world as much as it is to assist the student in making the mystical teachings have daily practical value in his or her life. The Rosicrucian Order seeks to enhance the student's relationship with the Master Within. The relationship should be developed to the extent that eventually he or she will feel perfectly comfortable going within, asking questions, being silent, and receiving guidance.

The Rosicrucian Order's teachings are profound, practical, beautiful, intellectual, mystical, and meaningful. They reveal the knowledge and ageless wisdom that governs the universe, and especially the physical, mental, emotional, psychological, and spiritual natures of our being. The Order does not seek to answer all questions and challenges regarding life. It seeks to lead the student to the source of all answers. The Order is committed to assisting the student in many ways during his or her progress along the path of evolution.

Through lectures, discourses, workshops, initiations, and rituals, the Order demonstrates, in the best possible way, an effective means of inspiring the Rosicrucian student to internalize and express in his or her daily life the wisdom that lies within the teachings. The Order seeks to inspire the intellect in such a manner that each person is motivated to create an inner commitment to these principles—principles that the human intellect may have already accepted through study of the monographs and participation in initiations and rituals. The Order accepts these challenges. Teachers and instructors assist and complement, but they cannot substitute for the knowledge and progress that can be gained through the monographs.

Practicing the teachings is the means by which the lessons of life are efficiently learned and not repeated in this or another lifetime. Practice is the principal method by which the soul personality evolves during this human journey. We learn through our daily experiences and relationships. Practicing the principles is the means by which cosmic laws are harmoniously learned and balanced in our lives, the means by which our debts are compensated and forgiven and our debtors receive understanding and compassion.

Through its teachings the Rosicrucian Order intentionally plants seeds of love, harmony, compassion, and kindliness into the consciousness. The fruits from this sowing may be harvested in this life, as well as in future incarnations, thereby fostering the progress of the evolution of humanity. The Rosicrucian Order also develops in students a desire to heal and bless others. Students learn to dispel apathy and not to hurt their brothers and sisters. Students learn to give a special kind of love: God's unconditional love. Students learn to see God within each person and in every form of life. They seek to look with love on everyone and everything. They desire to see individuals as they truly are—as unfolding soul personalities within the eternal soul of God.

Having been a member of the Rosicrucian Order for many years, I have received great inspiration and great strength, as have so many others, by focusing upon the pure essence of the Rosicrucian Order. We have always envisioned this essence as a lighted intelligence whose attributes include eternal and divine love, understanding, and wisdom. As we become aware of and attune to this essence, our consciousness is able to transcend the earth plane and material concerns, which include all human personalities.

In this state of transcendence, we become still and, bathed in cosmic light, envision the pure light of the Rosy Cross within this cosmic radiation. We stand in stillness, silence, gratitude, and receptivity. Without any effort or desire on our part, great spiritual personalities, once associated with the Order on the earth plane, are seen as they enter and remain in the light. While standing within the light with steadiness of mind and heart, these spiritual beings seem to radiate and transmit the essence of this divine light—the rays of which vibrate and descend to all humanity, the laws, love, and wisdom of the Cosmic. One of those entering and standing within the light is the spiritual personality of H. Spencer Lewis, not the man, nor the human personality, but a lighted spiritual personality. Many great spiritual beings before him are within this cosmic light, which infuses the Rosicrucian Order, sending forth light to inspire all Rosicrucians and all of humanity.

We solemnly plead that all join hearts and minds, and seek to attune to the cosmic essence of the Order's light, love, wisdom, and compassion. Standing thus within the light, may we invite these spiritual beings to transmit the higher energies of the Rosy Cross with increasing perfection into the consciousness of humanity and into all of life.

Our spiritual energies and the principles of the spiritual life, which we practice, will make their presence felt within all of our affiliated bodies and hence throughout the world. We are indeed the builders of a paradise on earth who externalize the kingdom of God that is within us. By realizing this and by dedicating ourselves to the essence of the Rosicrucian Order, we permit our thoughts to experience the presence of God. Through this practice, we train our being to become increasingly aware of God's spirit and love in all conditions and in all things—within us, within the members and officers of the Order, and within all humanity. We become conscious of who we truly are—spiritual beings, children of the universe, travelers of the universe.

One might say that we are evolving our ability to see and love the Order as God sees and loves it. We are the instruments by which God sees his creations. Our voices are the means by which God speaks to his creations, our ears are the means by which God listens and hears his creations. We serve as God's Hands and Hearts. Through us, God serves and loves all creations. So Mote It Be!

Let's Apply What We've Learned . . .

Exercise

(Read this exercise three times before performing.)

Become still. Quiet the body and calm the mind. Sit comfortably and relaxed in your chair. Close your eyes. Focus on your breath as you breathe deeply, slowly in and slowly out. When you breathe slowly in, hold the breath for a few seconds, and then breathe slowly out.

Still focused on your breathing, inhale, and silently say the word "*God.*" Slowly exhale sounding the word "*God*" again. Keep your center of attention on your breathing. Breathe slowly in, sound the word, and then breathe slowly out, silently saying the word. Continue this for two minutes or so, and then imagine and see your body as a body of pure white light.

Realize that your body is a temple of love and light. Keep this image and feeling for a few moments, then become still, silent, and passive. Become aware of any impressions. After a few moments, take three deep breaths and send love and light to all humanity. Take three more deep breaths and slowly return to the objective consciousness. Feel your feet upon the floor and your body seated in the chair. Give a moment of thanks, and then return to your activities.

"These lessons

bring us opportunities

to understand life's purpose

and for our progress

to happiness."

CHAPTER 7

Forgiveness and the Indwelling Soul

Forgiveness is a human and divine potential that lies within every human being. It is a divine art we all possess and are responsible for developing and utilizing. So why does forgiving seem difficult to us? What causes us to feel that by *not* forgiving, we strengthen and protect ourselves and thereby maintain power over the concerned party or condition? Do we think that when we forgive, we in some way lose our power? Do we imagine we must have the power in order to maintain the ability to assail offenders and make them feel guilty or obligated? What encourages us to feel justified in not forgiving? Is forgiving not appealing to us? You need to understand that we cannot truly move forward until we learn the process and power of forgiving.

If we truly understood the power of forgiveness and the positive effect it has on us, we would not resist it so strongly. Experiences of every sort are brought to us as learning tools in order that we might evolve in wisdom and understanding. By evolving, we become increasingly more conscious of our soul's purpose and of universal laws that govern human existence. Experiences are cosmic lessons designed by the soul and the soul personality. These lessons bring us opportunities to understand life's purpose and for our progress to happiness.

We cannot learn and evolve without experiences. People and conditions serve as cosmic role players, catalytic messengers, if you will, which assist in creating and providing lesson plans of experiences for us. Does it make sense to resent or to become angry with the messengers or conditions that provide us with experiences designed for our benefit? They might well be thought of as teachers. Our human consciousness may not understand nor feel comfortable with or like the experiences presented. Nonetheless, we are presented with opportunities to learn, expand, and grow. The human consciousness may not realize that we ourselves have helped formulate the experience.

The voice of the lesser self—the small self, the intellectual unenlightened human self, the ego—urges us not to forgive. The perception of the ego's reasoning claims and convinces us that it is too difficult to forgive and that we are justified in not forgiving. We must remember that the Divine Mind within us is all knowing and comprehensive in its knowledge of the past, present, and future. It does not reason in the manner in which our human intellect reasons. Hence, if your decisions are made believing only your human logic, rather than the inner Divine Mind, you are inviting limited decisions, which in turn invite a change in lesson plans and unexpected experiences.

Your knowledge, faith, belief, and trust should be in the soul and your inner Divine Mind. When we let our human logic create final answers for us, we fall out of harmony with soul purpose and with the True Self, as well as with the flow of universal intelligent energies, universal harmony, and universal life. We must not fail to practice and respect the All-Knowing Mind of the Master Within. Ignoring this Divine Mind brings life one disharmonious situation after another. When living in a world of "effect" rather than a world of "causation," inner peace diminishes and anxieties increase.

We must remember at all times that we are spiritual beings traveling on a purposeful human journey. The honest seeker on the path asks: "What is the pathway to forgiveness and soul consciousness? What is the pathway to freedom, liberation, and enlightenment?" We must bring this truth to our consciousness: God has given to every human being resources to make this journey one with meaning and purpose, a purpose consistent with God's law and the cosmic plan. The journey is filled with opportunities for spiritual growth and evolvement!

Our inner nature and the soul's wisdom govern the mystical pathway to liberation and freedom. It is a path of enlightenment revealing our true identity and the purpose of this reincarnation. You are urged to develop a relationship with the indwelling soul. It will inspire the mind and expand the consciousness, thereby bringing to you more and more the awareness of yourself as a *spiritual being*. Realizing and accepting this truth and keeping it in the forefront of the mind in all human relationships, you will attune to the intelligence and guidance of the soul. Your interpretations of experiences will be more comforting. This attunement helps us in developing a relationship with God and our true identity. This relationship assists in living a life that is more in harmony with nature and our fellow beings. It is your goal to make this relationship the single most important relationship of your life.

The intelligence of the indwelling soul aids in enlightening the intellect. Then we understand that our human experiences are responses to our choices, our thoughts, our intentions, and the actions we take. Our lesser self, our mundane mind with its intellectual analysis and encouragement from the ego, makes no connection between the human journey and our spiritual being. Some degree of enlightenment is necessary before this connection can be recognized. Until *light* is reflected into the human consciousness, the intellectual brain cannot make a conscious connection to the real self, the spiritual self, and to its purpose and goal. The ego urges us to disregard any signal or gentle prompting that may be sent from the soul.

We are all students, matriculating and registered in God's University of Life. Some of us are freshmen, some sophomores, others juniors and seniors. Still others are pursuing graduate degrees through special experiences. There is a common factor in all curricula. God has given each of us a special teacher, one who maintains connection with all the great masters. That spiritual teacher resides within us at all times. Enter into the inner private and special classroom that has been provided. While in the classroom, ask sincere and honest questions. Ask with and through the heart. You will receive guidance; follow the instructions. Seek to become aware of the lessons presented and commit yourself to contemplate and learn them.

"Right Relations" is an important lesson that is taught in the University of Life. Experiences encountered in relationships often require practicing the art of forgiveness. The spiritual teacher within aids us in learning the art of forgiving. Cosmic lesson plans are so designed that experiences are repeated again and again, throughout life, until the practice of forgiveness is learned. We are often offered excellent opportunities to acquire the skills and to practice the art and thereby grow and evolve spiritually.

There are six essential steps in acquiring the art of forgiveness. Each step requires contemplation, meditation, prayer, study, and continuous practice. Remember your special teacher within whose pleasure it is to guide and instruct you along the way.

1. Have an honest desire and commitment to forgive.

You must establish within your consciousness a true and unreserved desire to forgive. This requires that you release any sense of power or satisfaction which might be felt in a state of unforgiving. Accept and realize, in reality, that by forgiving, you are a beneficiary. I want you to know that in actuality, your body produces destructive neurochemicals that injure you physically, psychologically, emotionally, and spiritually when you hold unforgiving thoughts. Harboring thoughts of resentment, anger, and hurt, or thinking that you have been taken advantage of, is self-destructive. This is no longer purely a mystical statement of truth. Scientific research has demonstrated this same conclusion. Scientists have begun using the methodologies of basic research to investigate and demonstrate these biological, psychological, mystical, and spiritual laws. By holding thoughts of resentment, hurt, or hatred, you produce destructive neurochemicals that attack your immune system. Commit yourself to forgiveness and flood your system with constructive neurochemicals.

2. Visualize or imagine cosmic light and love within the person, situation, or condition that you are seeking to forgive.

This light is God's light, which is unconditional, and is not your light, which may have elements or conditions within it. This is a recognition that God is everywhere and within every person, within you as well as within the person who you are seeking to forgive and within the condition that you are resenting. Utilizing the most beautiful and perfect light that you can imagine as a symbol of God is a helpful technique in practicing the presence of God.

It is important that you develop an understanding of the spiritual meaning of light. Among many other qualities, God's light is full of love, life, understanding, compassion, wisdom, health, harmony, and an infinite number of other attributes. At this stage of forgiving, imagine cosmic light, which contains all the attributes of God—the brightest, purest, and most loving light imaginable—to be within and around the person, situation, or condition. Equally important is for you to see and feel the same light within and around *you*. God is light, and God's light contains all of God's love and creative power. By practicing the lighted presence, we evolve into a deeper understanding of not only our own soul and true identity, but also that of others as well. With this understanding we begin to live as spiritual beings and to utilize our spiritual faculties.

3. Seek cosmic understanding of the person, situation, or condition.

You must seek cosmic understanding of yourself. Go within and before the presence of your special teacher, desire to be given an understanding of the situation. While you are in silence and in the presence of the Master Teacher, release any preconceived ideas or feelings. Your pure and honest motives will be infused with universal understanding. You will gain a deeper view of life's experiences, of the person, condition, and of yourself. You may very well find yourself asking what you might need to understand yourself and what you need to change about yourself. Continue to go to the classroom about any specific matter until you are directed, inspired, or enlightened. The special teacher awaits and expects you. Understanding may come through a series of uplifting thoughts, readings, or feelings. There often arises a sense of thankfulness and self-discipline and an urge to utilize those uplifting thoughts in service to others.

4. Accept full responsibility for having first set the situation into motion.

Bring into your realization the fact that the law of cause and effect is always in motion. The creative laws, which govern our thoughts, intentions, motives, feelings, and actions, are always active. Show respect for these laws that are a part of your essence. We participate in these laws as karma/love, consciously or unconsciously. Our thoughts, desires, motives, intentions, and feelings are, in reality, not private at all, but a part of the universe. They radiate through cosmic law and seek to manifest as constructive or destructive, as "good" or "bad."

The original thought, motive, belief, or action has a vibratory effect upon the consciousness of the cells in our bodies. These vibrations grow, magnetize, and polarize our auras, and they in turn affect the nature and reality of our body, mind, and spirit. These radiations exert a magnetic pull that draws us to the experiences necessary for us to evolve. Also remember that the origin of all experiences that come to us is not entirely from this lifetime or from this source.

Do not judge or analyze the experiences of others as to cause and effect. In acquiring the art of forgiveness, we acknowledge the lessons or challenges which our experiences bring and the role that we are to play in our reaction to them. Universal or cosmic understanding (discussed above) helps to clarify this point.

Guilt plays no positive role in the evolvement of spiritual consciousness. Feelings of guilt need to be eliminated. The law of cause and effect is in reality also a law of love and not one of punishment. It is always designed to give us understanding and wisdom. The knowledge we acquire from each lesson will enable us to inspire and uplift ourselves and others. The law's primary motive is to refine us—to move us toward mastership. From the soul's perspective, no experience in and of itself is a "bad" experience. You may perceive it to be and create a negative reality from it; however, that is your doing. Remember the classroom within and go there for guidance, true understanding, and stillness.

5. Forgive yourself.

In light of the above comments, we realize what effect the external environment can have upon our perceptions; indeed, how it may color our judgment and influence our self-realization. We must begin the process of cleansing or purifying our consciousness so that there are no obstacles to the indwelling soul's work of developing the art of forgiving. We accomplish this by first forgiving ourselves.

Once you are free from all forms of guilt and self-deprecation, you become aware of who you are: a child of the Creator of the universe. As we continue to desire to forgive others and ourselves, and are dedicated to entering the silence of the inner classroom, we become aware of any dark corners in our mind. Some of these corners often harbor hidden feelings of resentment, anguish, or hurt. Practice forgiving yourself and others for all actions, known and unknown, as well as for thoughts or deeds from the past, present, or even the future.

Remember, true forgiveness is a process that occurs on the mental, emotional, psychological, and spiritual levels. Forgiveness will transmute and correct feelings and actions of the past, present, and future. Understand that the power to forgive is always present within you. It only requires your desire, honesty, sincerity, and prayer. We are then free to move forward to our higher good, and we aid others as they proceed to theirs. Do not focus on what you perceive to be your impurities; rather focus on the presence: the goodness within you, the God within, the Master Within. This will always bring a light that dissipates the darkness. Joy of the soul will sound forth.

6. Let go.

Let go completely. Your human personality must surrender its hold. Let the indwelling soul and the spiritual self emerge. All the force of intelligent love, of the universe, and the God Within will automatically guide you and inspire your thoughts and actions. The soul, God, and the cosmic masters will bring confirmation of your progress and the work to be done. The ego will no longer obstruct your spiritual progress. As you adjust to letting go, your knowledge, faculties, desires as well as your thoughts, intentions, and actions will progressively become more positive, constructive, patient, and loving. Your mental intention will seek to express the will of the indwelling soul, the will of God. Inwardly inspiration and comfort will grow. You will perceive a higher meaning to life's purpose and experiences.

While within the silence of the inner classroom, we are inspired and we visualize and create our realities with this inspiration. Repeat this process as often as needed. Your consciousness and repeated experiences will remind you if the job is incomplete. These reminders must not be interpreted as a lack of progress; rather, if you persist, the reward of spiritual growth will be great. Maintain your commitment to forgive.

Let's Apply What We've Learned . . .

Exercise to Practice Forgiveness

(Read this exercise three times before performing.)

Sit comfortably in a quiet location of your choice. With your eyes open, relax as you slowly and deeply take seven breaths. Pause for a few moments after each inhalation, then slowly exhale. As you breathe, turn your attention inward and begin to sense and realize the Presence of God. Keeping your eyes open, repeat the sound AUM three times, each time pronouncing the three component syllables (A–U–M) clearly and distinctly.

Close your eyes and imagine entering the personal classroom within. Your special teacher resides here, ready to assist and guide you. Enter this inner sanctum, your holy of holies, and take a seat. You feel safe, secure, and protected. You sense the presence of your teacher and you know that you have the intention as well as the capacity to forgive.

With this assurance, you begin to speak silently to the lighted presence within. If necessary, open your eyes and read meaningfully the following:

I intend to forgive;

I forgive all who have offended me;

Consciously and unconsciously, I forgive;

Within my heart and mind, I forgive;

From deep within and from without my being, I forgive;

I honestly and sincerely forgive everything in my past, present, and future.

I truly, earnestly, deeply, and with profound humility forgive everyone, every condition, and everything of the past, present, or future that needs forgiveness.

Everyone that I need to forgive is now forgiven;

And most of all, I forgive myself most sincerely and completely.

I am now free and all that I have forgiven are free. We all move on to our highest good. All is harmonious for us now and forever.

My mind, body, and spirit, including my immune system, are in harmony and are in Divine Order.

Having spoken these words into the creative mind of God, close your eyes and become still, silent, and receptive. After a few moments, take a deep breath and, feeling refreshed and enlightened, slowly and comfortably withdraw from your inner sanctum, your classroom. Sit for a moment with eyes open and then go about your activities.

" . . . live within this world

of limitless challenges,

diverse vibrations, and

complex relationships . . . .

You have chosen this as your path

of reintegration."

CHAPTER 8

An Inner Pathway to Reintegration and Mastership

*T*here is an inherent mystery in life—an inner urge, an attraction to move toward the light. This mysterious component of life is innate in all life forms. It is, one might say, an urge to seek illumination or to manifest the Creator's beautiful light. This urge is responsible for the interplay of human relationships and experiences. It is responsible for evolution's forward movement and progress toward the greater light.

Observe the plant pushing its way out of the darkness of the soil and into the light of the Sun where it can then express its full potential. Observe the infant, anxious to express life, moving and extricating itself from the womb of its mother under this mysterious impulse. Observe this innate urge in the human being as he or she continues the search for greater knowledge—greater illumination. Observe the human being moving into experiences and relationships that are destined to bring lessons to learn and thus spiritual growth. Observe the student of mysticism penetrating into the realm of the soul, a place of light and beauty.

Masters and philosophers have written on the pages of wisdom concerning the Book of Man and the Book of

Nature. This mysterious, governing intelligence is vibrating and communicating wisdom throughout all life. Behind the seemingly ordinary, routine aspects of our daily lives that constitute only the "appearance" of life, there is a mystery and a mystical existence.

If we are governed and caught up in the illusion of appearances, we only touch the superficial aspects of life and relationships. To become more spiritual requires us to create a desire to pierce beyond these veils of appearances and seek attunement with the reality that lies above and beyond the obvious. We seek to know the essence of spiritual realities or spiritual truths and to discover who we are and what is the soul's desire. The soul must eventually express itself through our human personality. If we were to contemplate and practice the truths of mysticism, we would achieve the realization of what truly governs life and events. The human form is a symbol, and eternal truths are veiled within all symbols. We would discover mystical wisdom by piercing and lifting the veil that lies within us and all around us. Cosmic laws and spiritual purpose are revealed at this point. Human experiences also often veil significant cosmic lessons and purposes.

As we learn to "read" symbols or grasp their true meaning, we acquire the techniques for "lifting the veils" and we enhance the process of regeneration. The soul begins to control the outer form of life and all of life's events.

Increasingly, we bring spirituality into our lives. Then, as true reintegration begins to take place, questions arise in the mind of the student: "How can I accomplish true reintegration? How can I learn to balance mystical teachings with daily experiences while living in a world full of crisis and conflict? How is this possible when I do not live a detached existence high on a mountain or in a secluded cave, away from the vicissitudes of life?"

Beloved, through the Law of Rebirth, you purposefully chose to live within this world of limitless challenges, diverse vibrations, and complex relationships, all of which have effects upon the body, mind, and emotions. For this reincarnation period, you have chosen this as your path of reintegration. You accomplish regeneration and reintegration by moving your consciousness further into the light. You also help in moving humanity forward.

Our daily lives seem to encourage us to forget who we really are and why we are on this human journey. However, it is our duty and responsibility to train ourselves to continually seek our true identity. It is our responsibility to seek and to understand the spiritual and the beautiful that surrounds us and is within us!

Petition by way of the heart to God and the cosmic host thusly:

O God, Thou Who art the Divine Architect of the Universe, Thy beauty that lies above and beyond the earth is like unto the beauty which I seek to perceive in my brothers and sisters and in all forms of life that surround me, whatever that form might be. Grant unto me Thine eye with which I might see this beauty. Subdue my human eyes whose tendency it is to highlight my brothers' and sisters' impurities and in so doing I have but strengthened my own imperfections. For if I am able to lift the veil and see the beauty that lies within my brothers and sisters and within all that surrounds me, I will be able to see and feel and express Thy beauty that lies abundantly within me. This beauty is all one and the same, one divine reflection of Thyself. We are all divine creations and spiritual reflections of Thyself.

As we enter the Aquarian Age, we are given the opportunity to find, see, and learn beauty in non-traditional forms and places. We must strive to discover beauty not only in the faces of all the people we meet, but in every manifestation of nature—in plants, trees, and flowers, in the waters, and in small and large creatures. We must also seek to find beauty in stones, driftwood, and even in a piece of scrap metal that has been artistically fashioned by the human hand and spirit. Spirit and beauty are in all these. The progress of regeneration and reintegration is the progress to unity. It extends and expands the consciousness to recognize beauty in all of life, in all people, and in all situations, no matter how difficult that may seem. You are intended to feel a unity with all of life, with all of existence.

Ask to see with the eyes of the soul. Such is the process of reintegration. The human eye is limited and fallible in its vision and perception. In the silence, ask for understanding and enlightenment. The indwelling soul will give you a vision of your unity with the Creator and will aid in expressing attributes of the Creator both *through you* and *as you.*

All of the above practices are intended to deepen our awareness of ourselves. Through this process we become more spiritual than human, and this reality is the means by which the valleys in your life will be exalted and the mountains and hills made low. The unstable and crooked will be made stable and straight. The challenges of life will become invigorating and will produce a state of balance. This is the means by which we bring about God's kingdom on earth and assist in manifesting God's will on earth as it is in heaven.

As we permit this light of the soul to permeate through us with increasing perfection, and begin seeing, feeling, believing, thinking, and expressing that eternal, beautiful, spiritual universe that lies behind and above all experiences and within us, we become liberated, reintegrated, and more spiritual. Each effort is a job well done and moves us further into the light of the Grand Architect's Plan with all of its rewarding and practical benefits.

The greatest work must be done in our emotional nature and psychic nature (henceforth, this emotional nature will be referred to as the "emotional body"). It holds the greatest challenge during our human journey as spiritual beings. The mystical process for accomplishing this is outlined on the pages of wisdom in the Book of Life. Many of you have accomplished much in this regard. It is important for you to become aware and conscious of all progress and make the commitment to continue.

Our emotional nature holds the greatest challenge during our human journey as spiritual beings. Just as the physical body has certain characteristics and functions, so does our emotional body. Early in human development, this emotional body is exposed to the vibrations, influences, and feelings of the external world. As a result, it develops an "open door policy" to external influences. Another way of stating this is that the undisciplined emotional body becomes a reflection of its environment. It takes on the colors, sounds, contacts, impressions, and movements from its surroundings and from anyone or anything that desires to enter. This emotional body becomes responsive to the outer world, to its desires, expectations, feelings, and, of course, emotions. These factors leave their characteristic imprints. Those with negative qualities create disharmony and confusion and may result in disturbing personality traits.

Sincere students of the spiritual path must continue progressively to seek and stabilize this important body. Efforts must be made to reorient the emotional body and to establish a guardian at its door in order that only harmonious events are welcome. The Inner Guardian grows stronger, and the "open door" policy changes. The emotional body ceases to react or to be disturbed. It now reacts only to higher mental, spiritual, and divine stimuli and from the prompting of the Master Within.

The path of regeneration and reintegration begins with a deep and honest desire for the Infinite. It proceeds through meditation and contemplation of the mystical, and through progressive initiations—all conditioned with an abundance of prayer.

Commit yourself to train and strengthen the emotional body. Much progress is made by utilizing the attributes of the mental/spiritual body. At this point, the Law of Thought takes hold and guides the traveler. Be consistent and patient in all of your efforts. The emotional body is destined to become as still and clean as a mirror, as well as serene and poised. As we walk between the Pillars of Opposites, we will be led to the path of balance and we will be able to transmit the light and love from the soul with increasing perfection. Practice "the silence" daily. Practice daily meditation and prayer. The consciousness expands as a result of meditation and it will radiate love and harmony into the environment and to all humanity.

Of course, as the process of regeneration occurs, our own imperfections and impurities are realized. Do not become alarmed, for they appear in order that we might expose them to the newfound light and understanding of our higher self.

As we acquire knowledge of the true self, and as we work to quiet the restless waters of our petulant emotions, we arrive at a state of imperturbability. Veil after veil will be removed. The once apparent differences among our brothers and sisters will no longer exist. Unity of mind and soul will be demonstrated. In harmony with this reality, all become as one, as we are meant to be. Our realization of oneness blends with the oneness of God; yet, we maintain our "individuality" within the Mind of God that surpasses all human understanding.

We offer seven "keys" to regeneration and reintegration. This message is for those students who dedicate themselves to continue on these mystical and spiritual paths, including the Rosicrucian and Martinist paths in particular. You are indeed among the chosen ones, a new community of servers to humanity. You are at the portal of a well-combined earthly and cosmic life. You are given certain eternal keys—ones that are in harmony with the Grand Architect's Plan that will make existence in this "new environment" balanced and harmonious:

1. Rededicate your efforts and life to your spiritual self, the Master Within, and to the oneness of life as if it were experiencing a new and exciting beginning.

2. Become very watchful, careful, and aware of your thoughts, beliefs, and motives. Be determined that they are constructive, positive, and designed to increase in harmony, peace, love, and spiritual consciousness. These objectives can be achieved through the use of prayer, visualization, meditation, and concentration. This will surely increase your spiritual stamina.

3. Seek to know the beauty, love, and accord that exist and flow through and in *all ways* and experiences in the world. Allow the "lighted oneness" to produce a balance and complete integration and alignment all through your life and being. Let it touch the heights and the depths, for at your stage of evolution and development "all ways" are fit and worthy now, and they are ready—with their colors, sounds, and vibrations—to be placed masterfully within the cosmic spectrum of oneness, into the cosmic keyboard.

4. Surrender the small self and all that you possess—psychologically and emotionally—to the One. Go within, and enter the "Light of Oneness" for total openness and inspection by the One.

5. For total openness and inspection by the One, dismiss the small self, with its limited perception and finite understanding, that brings to your attention disturbing events, news of misfortune, and negative impressions of every sort. These things throw you out of balance and harmony, causing you to sigh, become depressed, and wail and weep. This must stop!

6. You must move forward now without any trace of doubt, lest you place an illusion of an obstacle in your way. The heavenly floodgates are open, and all things shall come about for you, as you are faithful in love, truth, and purity to your higher self, God, and cosmic law.

7. You must go within and listen in the silence. Listen with awareness in the stillness. Relax your body, quiet the mind, and enter the Sanctum Within. Go there often and simply listen in that stillness to the One.

We leave you now at the portal of your new cosmic and earthly experience and existence. We feel quite comfortable in the knowledge that your journey will be creative, constructive, exciting, and invigorating, and that you will serve humanity as a co-creator of the earthly kingdom. This true work will enhance the unity of the soul personality and its experiences. This endeavor is the inner path to reintegration. Truly, we are experiencing reintegration. Dwell forever, my beloved, in the Eternal Light of Cosmic Wisdom.

So Mote It Be!

"I am a creative cause.

What do I desire

as one 'effect'

of my creation?"

CHAPTER 9

The Law of Cause and Effect
Karma and Reincarnation

*M*uch has been written and discussed concerning the Law of Cause and Effect. My intention is to highlight critical elements of these masterful presentations, training a spotlight on those that will particularly serve your needs. I picture those brilliant writings as being similar to a vast smorgasbord of well-prepared food. So many varieties of dishes are present that very little, if anything, can be added to this display. My goal here is to present essential mystical offerings in such a way that your conscious and subconscious digestive systems will be able to digest them and your inner system will absorb the essential nutrients, thereby better serving the needs of your body, mind, and spirit.

In order to do this effectively, I need your assistance. At this time, gently turn your focus upon your spiritual needs: the deeper needs of consciousness and that reality which will support and enhance travel along your present life's journey. This frame of mind is necessary so that you will not be overwhelmed by the smorgasbord's vast offerings, and you will be able to select and digest only those things that will fulfill your practical needs.

The Law of Cause and Effect is a creative law, basically designed so that you may create and experience a desired reality. This is a reality not only for your personal well-being, but coincidentally for the advancement of your fellow beings and humanity as a whole.

In this chapter, you will be encouraged to unite and blend the mystical concepts and truths that you may have previously accepted and known to be true for you. In your consciousness, these truths are isolated in individual compartments and are kept from uniting with each other as a whole. Their isolation prevents you from seeing how each one fits meaningfully with the other. When totally united into one whole, their union provides illumination, inspiration, courage, knowledge, and determination. The strength of their affiliation sets truths into motion and starts the active creation of your realities. You are to put into practice your newly found perspective. The spiritual universe provides the Law of Cause and Effect in order that balance (compensation) is maintained and actions eventually become purposeful in fulfilling the will of the Creator.

We have been told that decisions we make or choices we select need to be done with the intention of creating positive and constructive results. This requires us to operate from the "cause" side of the equation, the creative side. Think for a moment: "I am a creative cause. What do I desire as one 'effect' of my creation?" Keep in the forefront of your mind that you intend to be a creator of harmony, peace, and love. While still at the point of deciding and selecting a course of action, think: "How do I want to experience, feel, or think about the course of action I am about to take? I want to produce or create feelings of acceptance, not retaliation; goodwill, not resentment; accord and harmony, not disharmony or hate. Regardless of the 'effect' that someone, some condition, or cause may have delivered to me, and regardless of how impulsively my human (small) self wants to react, I still desire to be a creator of harmony, peace, and light. For I know that if I let go of these higher intentions, negative thinking and feelings will be returned to me tenfold, bringing chaos into my life. I also know that such negative thinking, however justified I may feel, will negatively affect the cells, neurochemicals, and immune protection of my body."

The quality of your thoughts determines the quality of your experiences. You choose to be proactive in your thinking and action and not to be reactive, for you realize that by becoming reactive, you become your own enemy and self-destroyer. You consciously and deliberately send thoughts and feelings of harmony, peace, love, and light immediately to people, places, or conditions, as difficult as it may be for you to do so at that time. At this very instant your soul, the Master Within, who has been awaiting your decision, will aid you in your "causative creation." You have passed the first requirement for matriculation in God's University of Life. You are destined to graduate as a Practitioner of Light. Practitioners of Light are co-creative with God.

You are to continue to digest inwardly, slowly, and totally the spiritual nutrients of this message. Each step of reading and contemplation brings its own reward. However, you will need more than a single reading or contemplation to acquire the wisdom in the above instruction and from the Master Within. Your life's journey will become exciting, challenging, and invigorating. Each attempt and step in reading and contemplation will bring its reward. Each contemplative effort will bring expansion and understanding of the spiritual laws that govern the universe and how you can cooperate with them and become a co-creator of reality. Be proactive and act upon your thoughts, feelings, beliefs, and motives accordingly. They all have the potential of creating harmony, peace, and love. Choose differently, or be reactive, and chaos enters.

LAW OF KARMA

Now, some brief comments about *karma*, which is no more than a great Law of Cause and Effect operating in a creative manner. I wish to make one thing perfectly clear about karma that is seldom emphasized in popular culture. A tremendous amount of the expressed energy flowing from the minds and hearts of humanity is good, constructive, selfless, and compassionate. These expressions have been responsible for bringing the "good" karma to humanity in the past and present; they will continue to do so in the future.

This good karma is responsible for much of what you enjoy daily through your five physical senses, as well as with your inner consciousness. Continue to do your part in contributing to good karma. How can you do this? By daily sending creative and causative thoughts of love, happiness, and peace, first into your personal environment, regardless of how limited or expansive it might be. Next, send these thoughts into the collective consciousness of all humanity. See yourself within the collective consciousness as a cosmic focal point, open to the flow of cosmic light and the radiating energies of cosmic beauty and love.

I suggest that you minimize your thinking of karma as bad, evil, punishment, personal disaster, or suffering. There is so much good karma that it more than neutralizes or offsets much of the bad. Understanding the Law of Karma and the Law of Cause and Effect, and subsequently attempting to harmonize with these laws brings about an understanding of how the effects of karmic law might be modified, mitigated, or neutralized.

Consider the Law of Gravity and how the study and understanding of this law has led to our ability to construct and fly airplanes, and then rockets, space shuttles, and even more. We often hear individuals urging others not to interfere with what they perceive as another's unfortunate karma. Unless one is advanced enough to understand all there is to know about the eternal journey of one's soul, we should always assume that it is possible to offer aid, support, and compassion to another by sending cosmic forces of healing, light, and love. Concentrate on the "good" karma that always surrounds the soul and do your utmost to channel cosmic healing and aid. As a result, "good" karma is created.

LAW OF REINCARNATION

I wish to make a few brief comments regarding the Law of Rebirth or Reincarnation, as this law clearly relates to and expresses the Laws of Karma and Cause and Effect, as well as other cosmic principles. My purpose in discussing specific aspects of this law is to give you some degree of understanding of the relationship of your present life to previous lives that you may have lived in the distant past. Practical interpretations will be offered to provide a deeper and more meaningful understanding of your present life's experiences. This in turn presents an opportunity to evolve more effortlessly toward mastership.

The Law of Reincarnation demands that all souls incarnate and reincarnate. Each human being is born into this life with a certain mission and with certain seeds or tools that are the products of past lives, endeavors, and experiences. Basically, this new life also brings with it certain deficiencies, incompleteness, and imbalances. All of these are to bear fruit of one sort or another. These Laws of Reincarnation and Cause and Effect are eternally and powerfully acting on each and every life. These laws dictate that "Whatsoever a man soweth, that shall he also reap," and that all must evolve.

In our present lives, the Law of Reincarnation veils and keeps hidden the secrets that lie behind our present incarnation. Human beings, either individually or collectively, come together to work out certain cause and effect (karma) involved in past lives. A true acceptance and understanding of this law should urge us to deal more fairly and carefully in our relationships with others. Every attempt should be made to perform duties and obligations whenever and however made. If the attempts are not made or made inadequately, obligations must be fulfilled at a later time or in a later life. Every seed we sow must bear the fruit of repayment.

Opportunities to forgive must be aggressively pursued. If not, the soul personality or the experience will reappear, and with greater consequences. Old friends as well as old enemies will seek contact in your life for resolution and growth. Be proactive and strive today to be just, kind, patient, and fair. Ask for guidance from the Master Within.

Regarding gender, every human being is incarnated cyclically as male or female. Specifically, men of today have been women in a past life, whereas women of today have lived as men. Cosmic law demands a balance of the negative and positive aspects of the lives of human beings in order to engender universal understanding and respect for all life. Sexual identity, as we know it, exists only in this human life form; it is not of the soul.

Men and women need to adapt a life of harmlessness toward each other and enjoy the benefit upon rebirth. Yes, one may correct, prevent, and transmute old mistakes by making a commitment to the state of harmlessness, to being loving, and to remaining proactive. Practice your soul's calling by becoming a practitioner of light and love, regardless of the situation you face and whether or not you consider yourself to be faultless in the matter. Make a daily habit every morning of announcing to yourself that you intend to be *harmless* on this day. Be determined to make it a day to look for the sacred and the beautiful in everything and in everyone.

So Mote It Be!

"Seek ever to

elevate and expand

your understanding

of love."

CHAPTER 10

The Law of Love

God of my Heart, God of my Realization, Father and Mother of every Soul, Thy Love that lies above and beyond the earth is like unto that Love which I perceive in all humankind—wordless and boundless. Grant unto me Thine Eye with which I might see that Love which lies within each individual. Subdue my human eyes whose tendency it is to highlight my brothers' and sisters' impurities, though by so doing, I but strengthen my own imperfections.

For, if I am able to see the Love that lies within my brothers and sisters, I will be able to see and feel Thy Love that lies within me, for they are both one and the same—One Divine Image of Thee. We are all One Divine Image of your reflection. So Mote It Be!

The Law of Love is one of the spiritual or cosmic laws that govern humanity and the universe. It is the basic law of creation. One perception regarding the purpose of the Law of Evolution and the purpose of life is to increase our capacity to love. Divine love dwells within all people. It is the underlying essence that determines the quality of our realization of life and beauty. The purpose of life intends for divine love to dominate our intelligence. Divine intelligence then unites with divine wisdom.

The Law of Love is little understood and poorly practiced. The Master Jesus enunciated this law for humanity as he encouraged us to love our neighbors as ourselves. We have not deeply understood and sincerely practiced this teaching. We must put forth effort and time to contemplate its meaning from a spiritual and practical perspective in order for the soul to reveal its wisdom. When we love only those who love us, or when love is only given to those from whom we expect love in return, our consciousness is overwhelmed by a state of selfishness. We are designed by our creator to love unconditionally. This spiritual law urges us to love others because within each person is the love of God and a divine soul that is essentially perfect. That same soul and God's love are likewise within us and make us as one.

Over two thousand years ago, Christ taught a selfless love. In order to avoid the effects of selfishness and disharmony, we should frequently ask ourselves, "Am I truly living and loving the best that I can? Am I seeking to receive God's unconditional love and radiating this love into my environment? Am I intending to love unconditionally and radiating this love to all those with whom I work, live, and come into contact?"

As students of a spiritual and mystical path, we no longer seek to criticize, resent, and hate or to use our powers for selfish purposes. This attitude allows us to offer ourselves as beacons of God's light and love. Our soul-felt intention will be to make our interpersonal relationships harmless. When we live and think from our higher mind—our spiritual mind—the resulting vibrations purify our environment and create an abode of harmony in our groups and organizations. Love for our group and organization will supersede any personal or personality desires. The Law of Love is the limitless power by which we rule the destiny of our lives. For it is the same power by which God rules the destiny of the universe.

To participate in serving humanity and rebuilding our civilization, we must mold our lives in harmony with this great Law of Love. Love unites humankind spiritually, mentally, and physically. It helps the weak to become strong; the strong, powerful; and the powerful, God-like. Love brings divine union between God and the universe, between God and humanity, and between a human being and his or her soul. This indwelling soul operates under the Law of Love. It allows us to see the beautiful that others might miss, and to miss the evil that others might witness and experience.

Love renders cosmic service that can only spring from a heart of pure goodwill. Love inspires us to be more tolerant, kind, caring, sharing, and respectful. It also prevents one from attempting to shape another being into one's own image. Instead, love engenders the desire to help the other person become his or her best or highest self. The ideal of our love evolves and brings with it a realization of God in all that is beautiful. It brings God into a greater realization. Love becomes a rainbow, bringing hope to life's cloudy skies, as our ideals are God-like.

Increase your willingness to forgive and to overlook the weaknesses of others. Send spiritual love and help to those who may have erred or fallen. These higher qualities bring nobility into your life and experiences. Seek spiritual values in human and cosmic contacts because this enhances our understanding and brings greater value to the spiritual side of life. Maintain a broad and tolerant perspective on all conditions and situations. As the principles of love are increasingly practiced in our daily lives, harmony and health increasingly enter our lives. Such a commitment will automatically establish a harmonious relationship with the soul. All negative interference by the small self will disappear, and the soul will begin to reveal and reflect itself without obstruction, through your human personality, blessing all with which it comes into contact.

Love is a far-seeing wisdom. It ever seeks to keep alive the impulse of God while providing for all a safe and secure progress. Love is guarding, caring, stimulating, and protecting. It expresses that affinity of souls which binds hearts together and draws them closer to God, thereby bringing heaven to earth.

When the heart beats with a rhythm of cosmic love and the head vibrates with cosmic wisdom, a connection is made with God and God's laws. That connection urges and beckons all into true cosmic service. Now the energy of love flows through, in, and about such service. All that we do will be harmless and good. Seek ever to elevate and expand your understanding of love.

Unconditional love brings a healing and soothing understanding that ignores mistakes. It recognizes no barriers or thoughts that separate and harm. Surround each other with that protecting wall of love which flows from the soul and which meets all physical, emotional, mental, and spiritual needs. At this time humankind needs a massive influx of love in action, for then world crises would be better understood, prevented, and dealt with.

When we internalize the teachings of the Christ, we advance individually and collectively. We eliminate many diseases of mind, emotion, and body. Christ's teachings, when actively practiced, make interpersonal, international, and national conflicts and wars impossible or more difficult to wage. By personally and collectively internalizing the Law of Love, we are able to reduce crime to a minimum, because the Law of Love provides limitless power and possibilities for those who are in attunement with it.

Those on the path are preparing for this work. As we express the precepts of love, we begin expressing divine feelings that honor and protect parents, children, loved ones, our animal friends, and indeed all living beings. We intend that our thoughts, actions, or words bring no harm to people, groups, or ourselves. We attune to the divine inspiration of love and speak words of devotion, as have the great poets, writers, and masters.

May the eternal stream of love which you are now receiving be permitted to continue on its journey by finding multiple paths through your being and into the hearts and minds of all humankind—blessing, soothing, enlightening, and strengthening all according to divine will, all according to divine law.

You are to assist in bringing God's light, love, and understanding back to earth—back into the collective consciousness of humanity, in order that it may give to the planet a new and refreshing fragrance, and to all of life a new spiritual beginning.

So Mote It Be!

"The great Law of Thought . . .

is the most fundamental,

for it connects

with other laws and influences

all of human

activities and experiences."

CHAPTER 11

The Law of Thought

As we become seriously committed to living a life that is physically, mentally, psychologically, emotionally, and spiritually harmonious, we find ourselves contemplating the many questions regarding life, as observed in ourselves and in others. What are the purposes and goals of life? What are the universal or cosmic causes for personal and group experiences that impact life? Are there causes and reasons for the varied and complex dynamics, both good and evil, observed in the world? Is it possible to be happy, loved, and prosperous?

I do want you to know that there is a path that can lead to an understanding of these and similar questions. This is the purpose of the profound mystical and spiritual teachings of the Rosicrucian and Martinist Orders. The path to wisdom has been announced and lighted by all the great avatars, teachers, masters, philosophers, and saints throughout human history.

This chapter is one of a series of essays that touch upon many of the questions proposed above, and also upon the laws by which the universe or the Cosmic governs. These essays are designed to stimulate that which is hidden within the consciousness, and also to plant valuable seeds capable of future growth. You provide the fertile ground upon which these seeds may fall when your desire to know is sincere and honest and when you are committed to spiritual evolvement. Keep your mind open and receptive. The growth of these seeds and the promise of a harvest will depend upon the efforts of tending and promoting their fruition through your consistent contemplation, concentration, meditation, humility, and prayer on a daily or periodic basis.

There are spiritual or cosmic laws that govern the universe and humankind. These divine laws were designed and created by God, the Divine Architect of the Universe, the Supreme Being, the Absolute, Omneity, or by any other name, path, or belief that one may wish to give to such an entity. If an individual is sincere in finding answers to the questions proposed, he or she will desire to become aware of and study these divine laws. With the knowledge, understanding, and respect of these laws, one could live in harmony with life and all events. This does not mean that challenges will not appear. However, if one is familiar with the laws involved and their application, the challenges can be invigorating, rather than defeating.

The great Law of Thought governs the spiritual universe. This law is the most fundamental, for it connects with other laws and influences all of human activities and experiences. This law functions through universal mind, which flows in, through, and about everyone. It is a creative intelligent power. Whenever we use our mind, we are setting into motion the creative power and energy of universal mind.

The universe is one complete, creative, and dynamic whole. All of our thoughts seek to manifest and become creative once placed into the universal mind. The quality and purpose of the emotion, intention, belief, feeling, and motive behind the vibratory energy released determines the nature of what we create. Every thought we think struggles to become a reality and is destined to manifest. Our thinking brings to us certain realities and experiences.

Thoughts are constructive and supportive, strengthening and capable of serving others, as well as us, when they originate from a desire of love and from the higher self. Thoughts of compassion can console the heavy heart when words cannot be found or are inadequate. Thoughts of a caring and loving nature can inspire, motivate, protect, and provide a sense of security, because they touch the soul and are in harmony with the creative urges and purpose of the soul and the universe.

The powerful law governing thought was written early upon the pages of wisdom in the Book of Life. Great masters and avatars have proclaimed this law and have translated and dispensed it upon every plane of consciousness. Since everyone thinks and everyone is a potential creator, whether realized or not, consciously or unconsciously, everyone uses the law and is affected by it. When the conscious mind produces a thought, it is delivered to the subjective and subconscious mind where universal law takes over and creation begins.

In the past, we have perhaps heard a great deal regarding this law and the effect of thought; however, perhaps two thirds of what has been heard has not produced a meaningful change in our behavior. I now wish to take the subject to still another level, bringing with it the essence of the first level. As we observe human behavior, we notice that a large number of people are not "self-thinkers." They are neither good nor bad—merely unthinking—and are entirely influenced and submerged in the "thought-world" of others. Nonetheless, they seem to be slowly evolving and moving toward developing an active self-consciousness and self-reality.

There is another group of people who are beginning to think independently and to activate and employ the laws of thought unselfishly. Most sincere students of mysticism might fall into this category. I would like to state that the proper use of thought is a learning process. It takes time, patience, and devotion. No person, regardless of how sincere and devoted, is free from failures or faults. Do not berate yourself over this. Only adepts and masters are free from these. What really counts are the upward and forward progress and commitment to improve.

Most students, if not all, are still somewhat selfish in some parts of their nature, prone to anger, resentment, ill temper, and irritability and, to a certain degree, hatred. Many times the predisposition to temper, irritability, and hatred come about by what the student may believe are "just" causes—actions that society may label as cruelty, hatred, or viciousness. Still other students may be subject to periods of self-doubt and depression.

Unacceptable intentions, actions, and destruction taken toward the planet as a whole or taken against animals, plants, or humans engender some degree of hatred, resentment, or anger. These are all called corresponding reactions. Instead of being proactive in response to such injustices, the good-intentioned person or student becomes reactive and thereby delays spiritual progress, bringing disharmony and chaos into his or her life.

Students of mysticism must learn to think proactively. We must put forth the effort to have both a positive mission and a focus in our thinking, to think correctly and not be forced into any thought-activity by reactions based on selfishness, ignorance, and lack of love, which have their seat or origin in the lower, emotional nature.

Proactive thought expresses attributes of the Creator-God: love, compassion, understanding, tolerance, and patience. Under certain circumstances proactive thought may seem difficult, and it is especially at those times when it is most important to think proactively. Reactive thinking has a "fight back" attitude; it tends to argue against a situation and is usually insensitive.

Reactive thoughts evoke chaos, confusion, hatred, and negative energies in the "enemy." Learn to be proactive instead of reactive. Proactive thoughts are thoughts of CAUSE and invite constructive, creative, and supportive cosmic energies. Under all circumstances, we must remember that "we get what we give." Whatever thoughts, ideas, and beliefs we put into the creative mind, the Law of Thought will then return the idea back to us in demonstration.

There are always apparent exceptions. A highly devoted individual, who has been divinely empowered to do a certain work, may evoke feelings of hatred and also reactions (that cause the devotee much trouble) from those who do not understand this work and those who cannot see, or refuse to accept, the constructive and beautiful end result. Devotees must perceive any reaction they receive as impersonal, even though the reaction seems to focus on the individual. The reaction comes about because they represent an idea, and the idea creates a certain effect in the recipient.

A thought or idea results from the impulse of an emotion that is a response to a particular desire. This motivating energy activates the mind and might be positive or negative, selfish or unselfish. Affirm that all your motivating desires originate with positive, constructive, and selfless intentions. Keep in mind that the thought's vibratory energy, once created and constructed, will remain in the aura and form a vibratory magnetic wall completely surrounding the body and producing its thought-aura. This thought energy increases in strength as such thinking continues, growing until it creates its own reality.

Negative creative thought energy has the potential of becoming more powerful than its creator. The individual becomes obsessed by his or her own idea and is driven by its creation. One can glean from the law that spiritual, loving thoughts—thoughts of harmony, peace, and cosmic guidance—can fortify, support, and protect the student or the associated group.

Creators of thought vibrations, regardless of whether these thoughts remain in the aura or radiate outward, become involved in the Law of Karma. These thought vibrations are children of their creation. Hence, the student must guard against creating a negative thought that expresses any likes or dislikes. One should not use the energy of mind and thought to make possible the desire that originates solely in the personality. Such must originate from the soul. Every sincere student should adhere to this.

I wish to touch upon another form of thought energy that I have found to be prevalent and one that causes much trouble, especially in local group activities and larger organizational work. Personal matters that concern groups of people are not exempt from the effects of this type of poisonous energy. I am referring to so-called facts and information—the news, if you care to call it so—the basis of what usually degenerates into gossip. Such thoughts may concern the lives of participants in ritualistic work, in business, management, or even in making adminis-trative decisions.

For example, a person may come to you and relate a fact of so-called wrongdoing concerning someone or some situation. Being a sincere Rosicrucian student and com-mitted to preventing any mental poisoning, you will realize that the so-called wrongdoing may be something that is wrongly perceived or perhaps of a karmic nature. It may in itself have a good and positive motive. You are faced with a choice, the result of which will produce consequences. You may either hand the information to another, and thus put it into endless circulation, or you may make a firm decision to not add to the conversation and stop it here and now with you. With you, it has come to a dead end.

Visualize cosmic light and love flowing through you, stopping this negative energy from circulation. Let an abundance of cosmic love stream forth through you to the alleged erring person or circumstance. An abundance of love, understanding, strength, and knowledge flows, along with inspiration for grasping and applying the lesson to be learned through the person's experience. You must not use force to do this, for you know that you must never unduly influence another's mind. Let gentleness and wisdom guide you.

Gossip and destructive words can be broken into pieces by the power of a counter-thought of unconditional love, peace, and harmony. Do so with a gentle stream of warm compassion. To carry this out successfully requires discipline and a dedication to the soul and to the Master Within. Petition to be free of any ancient habit that you have carried from one incarnation to another. Be determined to clean your slate. Start the process now. Your plan is eternal.

The masters have taught that strong negative thought vibrations act as boomerangs, returning their energy to the sender with increased velocity. Likewise, strong thoughts of hatred or resentment can return charged with the energy of the hated person unless they are neutralized by strong thoughts of light, love, and forgiveness.

Take care not to permit your mind to transmit to another person "facts" or untruths of a negative nature that may have originated in the resentful, emotional, or undisciplined mental nature of another person. Your choice is between vitalizing the information received or arresting it. The thoughtful and spiritually oriented person will arrest it with cosmic support of the true union. The action of restraining negative thoughts renders the thought vibration harmless. Cosmic law sends it back to the originator with cosmic power that may disintegrate it. In returning it harmlessly to the sender, the emphasis is on *harmlessly.*

How can sincere students progress along the path of evolution and guard against unwanted experiences? How may we correctly build a strong, positive, and loving mental aura to surround and sustain ourselves? How might we increase our mental and spiritual contact with the soul and with the souls of our fellow human beings?

The first step is to understand the meaning of harmlessness and to commit to its practice applying harmlessness in thought, motive, feeling, speech, and action. Make the commitment to yourself and to your soul to lose any addiction or craving for careless, critical words of any sort. Make the determination not to attack anyone with criticism, however disguised. Understand that by no means is harmlessness related to weakness or sentimentality, nor is it merely avoidance of discomfort. Eliminate and resist thoughts of "getting back" or retaliation towards those who seem to offend you. Patterns and old habits of thinking should be reviewed in light of your new commitment to become constructive and creative in your thoughts and actions. Harmlessness involves constant activity and cultivation. It is a process. Be patient and yet persistent with yourself.

From the light of your soul, reexamine preconceived attitudes and feelings about persons, situations, places, or conditions. Make a determination to become harmless and to have a positive attitude by being strong and considerate. Be patient in developing this spiritual art, for it does not come quickly or without constant watching. Harmlessness will develop, and when it does, what a great reward and accomplishment it is.

The harmlessness discussed here slowly develops with a control of the human personality by the soul. This leads to an attraction to the world of ideas, for ideas are the abode of the soul. One's mundane thought world loses its primary control. The student learns to function in both the world of ideas and the world of thought through the practice of meditation and "the silence." Through harmlessness, one has developed the capacity to perceive the consciousness and reality of one's spiritual companions; forgiveness is complete and the capacity to support and nurture is born.

When our powerful emotions originate within the undisciplined personality, they are ill conceived. Nevertheless, they are also still creative and can produce harm.

Harmlessness must be introduced and developed as an expression through our emotional and mental nature. As love pours forth from the soul, it alchemically transforms the undisciplined emotional and mental nature into a state of harmlessness. The student who commits to such an admirable path will be cosmically supported and will acquire access to all the inner resources of his or her being. Patience, meditation, contemplation, prayer, time, and effort are required. The benefits and karmic response resulting from such efforts will be well worthwhile. As a result, the self evolves, and spiritual development becomes strong enough to exercise positive effects upon those with whom contact is made—those who are in one's world and within one's environment.

Become aware of all of your thoughts in terms of polarity and vibratory quality. Let conscience guard your doorway of thought. Carefully supervise and cultivate your thought life. Affirm that certain lines of thought will not be permitted nor received from others. As these outside thoughts appear, reject them and tell them to "Begone!" Do not allow them entrance into your temple. Live in the thought world of your higher self and open your mind to the influx of cosmic ideas. Add resources to your warehouse: reading, study, contemplation and concentration, and "silence." The world of ideas is the world of the higher mind.

Always desire to become conscious first of your soul, and from that state of consciousness, desire that it be in charge of your life and all of your affairs. Think not that life is without design or ill-planned. Life is the flowering of your thoughts, the very product of your hands.

Your thoughts constitute your prayers. Use thought and belief to create your realities wisely. Do not create thoughts that produce the illusion of limitation. Instead, create thoughts that expand and extend for you that which you desire to expand and extend. Create thoughts that heal and bless you and others.

Peace, joy, and light will be with you as you remain faithful to your divine resource.

So Mote It Be!

(Please see "Let's Apply What We've Learned" on next page.)

Let's Apply What We've Learned . . .

Exercises for Practicing the Principles of Love, Harmony, and Fellowship

(Read silently or aloud three times before performing.)

If the devoted student sees a need for a true expression of love, harmony, and fellowship within a group, he or she can accomplish much by silently beginning a process that will have the capacity to manifest exactly what is desired. Here are the necessary keys:

1. Commit yourself to being God's source of light and love in all of your relationships within any group.

2. See yourself, imagine yourself, and visualize yourself each day as a lighted being of cosmic light and love. See cosmic light and love descending to and through you as you hold still within this light, absorbing, reflecting, and transmitting its energies. Hold this picture for a few moments at any time in your sanctum or at any other time that is convenient.

3. Before attending any group, imagine yourself as that light. Imagine walking into and among the group, radiating and receiving cosmic light—blessing all you see.

4. Radiate unconditional love intentionally, deliberately, and periodically. Do not permit appearances to interfere with this feeling of light. This feeling should not prevent you from conversing and carrying out your regular activities in the group.

5. During a period when you are physically away from the group, see the space that the group occupies as a place of light, cosmic light—as if the Sun itself were radiating its brightness and love throughout the space.

6. See people drawn to this light and receiving cosmic blessings as it bathes and refreshes all that enter into its radiance. See everyone who enters being refreshed. All worries, anxieties, and burdens are removed. You observe people leaving with joy and happiness upon their faces and in their minds and hearts. Make this cosmic contribution to yourself and to all of life.

"... to perceive the wordless and boundless intelligence communicated and symbolized ... one should elevate the mind and consciousness away from material realities."

CHAPTER 12

The Eternal Symbols of Light, Life, and Love

*S*chools of mysticism place great emphasis upon understanding the importance of their rituals and initiations. Likewise, the words *Light, Life*, and *Love* are frequently used in mystical initiations, rituals, and writings. The purpose of this chapter is to elevate our consciousness so that we might reach another level in both our search for Light, Life, and Love and in our discovery of personal meaning in mystical words and symbols, for as we progress in our mystical studies, we will continually discover ever more profound meaning in familiar words and symbols.

Humanity's early history reveals that symbols and signs have been utilized as a means for conveying thoughts and ideas or to express an exalted unknown. Symbols have served as excellent catalysts in expanding consciousness and moving it toward the spiritual. One might say that the use and purpose of symbols is to represent with a visible or audible likeness that which cannot be completely communicated or understood by our five physical senses.

Great archetypal symbols have always generated a hierarchy of interpretations, and to imply that there is only one definitive interpretation of a particular symbol is to limit the possibilities of the human experience and consciousness.

Through contemplation and meditation upon a mystical symbol or word, harmonious cosmic attunement is established and experienced by the inner faculties. When mystical intuition is brought into play, inspiration and enlightenment are received and expressed within the emotional and psychic self.

Relaxed concentration and visualization of the many shapes or forms that a symbol may assume will help attune the seeker to what lies behind, above, or within that symbol.

Written and spoken words are also used symbolically in mystical settings. These often veil mystical truths and eternal laws. The words *Light, Life,* and *Love* are often used in mystical rituals and initiations. These words are imbued with eternal and divine meanings. In order for us to perceive the wordless and boundless intelligence communicated and symbolized by these words, we should elevate the mind and consciousness away from material realities. The mind should be passive and receptive, while at the same time expressing an attitude of relaxed expectancy.

All rituals and initiations should be approached as if they were being experienced—seen and heard—for the first time. Become childlike and patient in your controlled desire to understand, receive, partake, and comprehend any eternal wisdom that might be impressed upon your consciousness. In such surroundings, while the physical senses and faculties are still utilized, their use is somewhat subdued, and the inner, higher, spiritual faculties are elevated and permitted to participate in the experience. Gently ask within for these faculties to *see* and *hear* for you.

While Light, Life, and Love are part of all that we naturally see and experience, they are veiled or hidden by our attention to the material and the mundane. The mystical student's intention is to remove, one by one, these veils so that, to some degree, a greater realization will appear. For although Light, Life, and Love are obscured, in removing the veil, a realization dawns that *Love*, for example, gives birth to all that is good and renders purpose to that which is named "Beauty." Love is boundless and eternal, and it assures continuity in the expression of all experiences.

Love creatively expresses itself both horizontally and vertically. Its horizontal expression creates the means by which the soul evolves during its earthly journey. It reaches out to all humanity and all of life, bringing harmony to all. Love strengthens, enlivens, supports, and nurtures the spirit of humankind.

In its vertical expression, Love moves deep within, where it realizes a union and oneness with God. With this realization, Love ascends and expands upward throughout the heavens, and is aware of its kinship with all the stars, planets, and worlds. Love's innate desire is to return home again and again to experience the bosom and embrace of God—pulsating within all the souls who have journeyed there to become "supreme lights" within the greater light of supreme beauty.

Then there is *Light*, which is an attribute of God and creates that which manifests through the Rose. The Rose unfolds only in the presence of Light. Responding to the Light and the Cross, the Rose absorbs, reflects, and transmits its evolved Light.

Light creates and manifests everything, even the Rose, giving purpose to the Cross, and thereby unfolding the Rose.

Light is that which gives understanding and makes visible eternal truths which, when revealed and honored, expand the consciousness, thereby making it capable of perceiving ever-greater realities. Light exerts and expresses effortlessly its power to dispel darkness wherever it enters and to whomever turns in its direction.

Finally there is *Life*, existing and moving invisibly through all that *is* and all that *expresses*, and in all that becomes visible and invisible. Life manifests on earth, as it exists in heaven—visible and invisible, known and unknown. It is life that permits breathing and provides cosmic rhythm to all that vibrates. Life causes soul to smile with joy; it shines forth, revealing and elevating beauty to a place beyond pleasure, to one of gratefulness, adoration, gratitude, and kinship. Life's eternal mission is to return again and again, bringing ever-increasing perfection. It causes the Rose to exist eternally. The seed of the Rose returns again and again upon the Cross. The Rose finally absorbs within itself all that the Cross contains and offers. It then becomes one with the Infinite Creator of all lighted, unfolded Roses. Life proclaims an existence that is everlasting and without beginning or end. Thus, another level is reached in searching for and expanding upon the symbols of Light, Life, and Love.

So Mote It Be!

"There is a plan

and purpose

for humanity

and for human evolution."

CHAPTER 13

The Plan

*T*hroughout mystical literature, including the Martinist and Rosicrucian teachings, we find reference made to a Divine Plan and the Divine Architect. The term *Divine Architect of the Universe* implies that there is a Divine Creator or Builder. We can further assume that the Divine Architect of the Universe has a glorious and magnificent purpose. The great masters, avatars, and the hierarchy refer to this divine purpose as the Plan—the Divine Plan. An architect creates plans to be carried out and accomplished. As students of mysticism, it is also reasonable to assume that we individually and collectively have the capacity to know attributes or manifestations of this magnificent Plan.

We are all workers of the Divine Architect, the Absolute. Our responsibility is to attempt to perceive directions and guidance by doing our part in putting the components of this divine structure together. In reality, our higher selves, our true selves, are the component workers, which are to form, manifest, and comprise the architectural structure of the Plan.

What is this universal plan of the Divine? Can we know exactly what the Plan is and our relationship to it?

The Divine Architect is infinite in its being, and we cannot define infinite beings. Neither can we know or define the Infinite Plan. How then may we gain a realization of the Plan and become conscious, willing workers and participants in it? Participation in the Plan may be conscious or unconscious. We strive to become increasingly conscious participants. The journey, which leads to knowledge of the Plan, is the journey that leads to knowledge of *self*. One must seek the doorway of the Master Within for this wisdom.

One point should be made perfectly clear in the beginning: There is a plan and purpose for humanity and for human evolution. One may gain a realization of the Plan by becoming aware of some of the Plan's attributes, qualities, laws, and purpose which govern its revelation or evolution. The degree of conscious apprehension of the Plan will necessarily vary according to the student's progress and response to the energies of evolution and growth. Our response to evolution dictates the level of consciousness and wisdom acquired. All points of evolution and levels of consciousness are essential and important and all levels of apprehension of the Plan serve. Some levels have greater responsibilities than do others.

Participation in the Divine Architect's purpose for humanity, individually and collectively, is through response to "lesson plans" that are presented through all human experiences, relationships, circumstances, and affairs of life. These are designed to produce illumination and expansion of the consciousness. The expanded consciousness will enable the student to discern the attributes of soul and the higher self. Once the attributes of the spiritual self and its mission are realized, there will automatically be a strong urge and commitment to the will of the soul. This commitment brings about changes in life as expressed in the material environment. These changes will be in harmony with spiritual laws that govern the universe and are in harmony with the Divine Plan.

The attributes of the Plan are revealed within the inner self. There follows an internal commitment and effort to spiritualize the expression of the human personality in the material world. A spiritual infusion takes place in all human activities and groups—political, economic, scientific, religious, artistic, and healing. Along these lines, this same infusion can bring about the spiritualization of money, for example. By the infusion of this purpose, more money is made available for the work of the Divine Architect and the hierarchy. The soul then begins to control the outer form of life and all events.

Three different approaches can be taken in bringing about a realization and manifestation of the Plan. The first approach is by continuing on the path to an understanding of who you truly are, and becoming aware of and identifying with the attributes and qualities of the *true self*. This is fundamental to advancing on the path and expressing its spiritual and mystical nature. A great deal of inner light will begin shining through the personality with the dawning of the realization of who you truly are. I urge you to give attention to this part of your being every day. Contemplate its meaning and visualize its manifestation and attributes.

One way to accomplish this is to ask, "What are the attributes of light?" After contemplation and meditation upon this question, make a list of these qualities. Place this list of attributes where you can think about them and be reminded of them daily. Contemplate these attributes one by one. Each of these is also an attribute of the true self and includes: cosmic light, unconditional love, cosmic understanding, harmony, peace, joy, compassion, oneness with all life, unity with all souls, equanimity, grace, wisdom, strength, courage, kindliness, forgiveness, beauty, animate and inanimate beauty, humility, and giving as well as receiving. These attributes are of your true self! Know this. You will no doubt be led to add to this list as your attunement grows. As you contemplate these attributes one by one, start to embody each one of them.

In contemplating each attribute, realize that you are truly that attribute, and then will yourself, daily, to externalize that attribute with increasing perfection. Commit yourself, in some small way, to living more and more as your true self—living as who you truly are.

You will gradually and progressively withdraw life from the false self, the ego, and will cease expressing and living the life of the lesser self. As you do, the soul will begin to take charge of your life. Practice this, and notice the changing patterns of your thoughts and feelings. This will bring an awareness of the quality and nature of your thoughts. If any thoughts fail to harmonize with the qualities of the true self and its attributes, the higher self will gently urge you to reject and neutralize them by expressing thoughts of love, light, and caring.

By following this process, the physical brain will gradually develop pathways to correctly perceive and interpret messages from the soul. The mind will assume the function of transmitting to the brain the desires and will of the indwelling soul. The human personality becomes more beautiful as it now reflects and transmits the beauty of the soul's urges.

As you contemplate your true attributes and make a commitment to try daily to express them, you will be enhancing and building the most important relationship in your life: your relationship with soul personality and universal soul. You will gradually, slowly, and inwardly begin to perceive attributes of the Architect and the Divine

Plan. One cannot realize the Plan until a relationship with the true self is established.

Within each personality is a potential, specific part of the Plan. This part is to be worked out, developed, and manifested through *you*. Remember, your mission is to evolve and advance throughout this present incarnated life. There are no big or small parts of the Plan. You determine your involvement in the Plan by your awareness, evolution, choices, and cooperation with the indwelling soul and soul personality. All workers are important to the Divine Creator.

The second approach to bringing about a realization of the Divine Architect's Plan is through attunement with the Architect's major engineers; the great masters and sons and daughters of God, who expounded and taught the laws and truths that are fundamental to the Plan. Two of these great engineers are the Buddha and the Christ. They taught and demonstrated great and inspiring lessons to humanity.

Buddha's task was to supplant ignorance with true knowledge. Ignorance produces hindrances to building, evolving, and walking the inner path. Ignorance results in wrong habits and practices of thought and action, and the misuse of the laws that govern thought and the thinking processes. Buddha taught pure reason as an approach to the inner divine self. He brought illumination to the world and embodied the principles of wisdom and light.

We often hear and read the words *love* and *light* in our mystical studies and rituals. Take the time to contemplate and meditate upon the deeper meanings that lie behind and above these word symbols and phrases. What do they symbolize? What silent wisdom are they trying to communicate? Do you feel that your present understanding of these words constitutes their ultimate meaning? Are you striving to pierce, veil by veil, the mystery and wisdom of the eternal meaning of cosmic light and unconditional love? Remove any impediments from your mind that prevent you from entering the hall of wisdom and illumination.

The human consciousness generates a light that is commonly used in dealing with everyday, commonplace problems. This lesser, mortal light is intellectual and tends to be self-limiting, self-generated, and self-exhausting as it communicates beams to influence persons and conditions. This mundane light highlights appearances and illusions in the consciousness. It does not contain the higher vibratory energies that are capable of revealing true realities. True wisdom and reality lie behind and above the world of appearances. They bring harmony and peaceful conditions to relationships. The light of the soul eliminates illusions and sees behind, through, and above appearances. The qualities and vibratory nature of the light of the soul include revelation and illumination. This light promotes reintegration and regeneration. Its consciousness is in the eternal *now*.

The soul is essentially a being of light and love. Its light constitutes the true medium for universal mind. The soul is symbolically similar to the Sun, since the "rays" of both soul and Sun pour out into the darkness. The rays of the soul pour out into the darkness located within the mortal consciousness of humanity, illuminating and radiating throughout the human personality, so that person's life truly begins to express its spiritual likeness.

Solitude is a condition that cultivates our consciousness to gain a realization of the Plan and to serve the Divine Architect. Contemplate the meaning and purpose of solitude. This is a time when God speaks.

When in the midst of a troubling experience, quietly and mentally withdraw the mind from thoughts, emotions, and desires of the world in which you live and work. Withdraw from these: let them go. Silently and quietly center the consciousness in the world of the soul and be still. Patiently open windows of the mind and consciousness. Wait *in the stillness of the lighted presence*. Remain silent, knowing that the light of God and the soul shine gently upon you, illuminating the dark corners of your mind. Let illumination take place. Surrender. Guidance and direction are received in the silence.

Illumination and the light of knowledge are synonymous terms. Illumination and the perception of truth are also one and the same. The quality of our perceptions determines the quality of our thoughts and actions. Determine and pray that your perceptions are true. Develop the art of using the technique of the light of the soul.

The great engineer and son of God, Buddha, perceived and embodied the Divine Architect's principle of wisdom and light. The other great engineer of the Plan, the Christ, brought the principles of love to humanity and embodied in Christ was a great cosmic law: the *Law of Love*. Just as with other universal laws, the Law of Love is inadequately understood and practiced. The Christ encouraged us "to love our neighbor as ourselves." We are to truly seek understanding of this enunciation through the practices of contemplation and meditation.

A large percentage of humanity is centered in a state of being where the full extent of their love is merely to love themselves and those who love them. The masters taught that we should love our fellow human beings universally, unconditionally, and truly. When we meet and seek to relate to other people, we must especially bear in mind that everyone has a soul, a divine nature, that is essentially perfect—a soul just as our own. Focus on the fact that they are traveling both a human and an infinite journey, just as you are.

Begin to see and relate to fellow beings as souls, and not as mere physical entities. Two thousand years ago, the Divine Architect's greatest expression of love taught this principle and lived it. Let us pause for a moment and inwardly ask in silence: "Am I truly as loving as I could and should be? Do I really understand the power of love? Do I know how to love? Do I know how to send God's love to another? Is my love unconditional as is God's love, or do I send my love with some conditions?" Ponder with sincerity each one of these questions. God and your soul will assist in finding the answers and guide you to the art of loving.

Love has the power to negate poisonous thoughts created by you or by others. Make the right choices and bring health, joy, happiness, and peace to yourself and to others. When sending resentment and hate seem so "natural," make the choice of sending love instead. Petition for God to send love to and through you to the person, place, or condition when the small self is calling on you, with the intensity of its feeling, to be revengeful and judgmental.

Observe your hesitations and answers to the questions above and note the work you are silently committing yourself to accomplish. Attune with your soul, for it knows how to assist you so that you can finish this work in your present incarnation. Remember that the art of loving is an eternal far-seeking wisdom, bringing with it much good karma. The reverse may be true as well, when we choose unwisely and miss an opportunity to love.

As we internalize the teachings of the Christ, we will individually and collectively begin to become more and more inclusive in our ability to experience love and compassion in all relationships. We become aware of God sending love and caring to us through the people with whom we come into contact. As a result, we give thanks to God for sending love through us to all those with whom we relate.

Practicing the art of loving may appear to be difficult at times; however, we who are on the path are up to the task. We may paraphrase Christ's teaching by saying, "Let me live a life that is harmless in every way, and loving, and giving in every discord." By practicing this great engineer's concept we learn that our thoughts, actions, or words are vibrating at such a divine frequency that they will only bring love and peace to ourselves and to all people.

The laws that the two great engineers and sons of God, the Divine Architect, taught are part of a plan to bring a realization of heaven on earth. For behind these laws are the power and laws of the Divine Universe. Humanity's realization of the true validity of these laws is merely a matter of time, for evolution must produce realization eventually. The forming of an earlier recognition lies within our hands.

In conclusion I will only mention very briefly the third approach to a realization and participation in the Plan. The hierarchy might be regarded as custodian of the Plan for humanity, and as such impresses the minds of those who are prepared and dedicated with ideas and information. If these are correctly perceived and acted upon, they will bring about a degree of realization, evolution, and support for the Plan. Mystical intuition enables the student to be receptive and attuned to cosmic impressions and guidance.

What greater plan can there be but to bring a realization of heaven within us and on earth and to have the soul express with increasing perfection through our human personalities? In this manner the material world becomes spiritualized and proclaims the Kingdom of God as a reality in the hearts and minds of humanity. The attributes of the kingdom and the attributes of the soul are one. They lie within each of us. May the light, love, and power manifest God's Plan within and through each of us. You will then dwell within the light of cosmic wisdom.

Close this reading with the following invocation. As you read these words aloud, let them resonate within you as your own words, spoken to the universal soul within you.

O My Soul,
Who dwells within as an Eternal
Source of Love
Grant unto me your Eye that
I might see the Beauty that
Surrounds me.
Grant unto me your Ear that
I might sense and hear your
Soundless Voice.
Let your Light and Love
Radiate through and from me
That I might serve humanity and
All of Life. All to the Glory of God.
So Mote It Be!

May you ever dwell in the eternal light of cosmic wisdom.

"This is a beautiful

planet with beautiful,

loving, and caring

people."

CHAPTER 14

A Call for Healing and Peace

*B*efore reading this chapter, please take several deep breaths, breathing slowly in and slowly out. Then center yourself, drawing unto yourself the attitude that you are in the very presence of God. Sit relaxed for a moment and then read the following invocation silently or aloud:

God of our Hearts, as students of Thy divine and mystical laws, quiet the sounds of fear, grief, sorrow, depression, hate, revenge, and anxiety which come to our hearts and our minds, and to our eyes and our ears.

Raise our consciousness above these clouds—higher, higher, still higher, until we are once again within Thy Light. For Thy Light is Intelligence, so full of constructive purpose and understanding. While within this Light infuse our being with Thy meaning, love, wisdom, and understanding, that we may transmit these by means of spiritual service into the hearts and minds of all humankind . . . to all of Life. Have us know that within our being are Your Peace and Your Power, Your Love and Your Understanding.

So Mote It Be!

In trying to communicate to you the message within my consciousness, my desire is that you sense and feel the invisible divine or spiritual energy that flows through the written or spoken word, and which flows through these words that you are now reading.

In these times, marked by disturbances, confusion, agitation, and violent disorders among many people and nations, which our consciousness is now experiencing, I want to make one thing perfectly clear: The state of humanity is sound and humankind is rapidly awakening. And although there is much that needs to be changed and much more work yet to do, all pessimism regarding the planet's future must be stopped and transmuted by means of light and understanding.

We read and listen to the news that continuously reports destructive acts of nature and humankind's violence, crimes, and abuses. Every day we see and hear of acts of terrorism and atrocities. These deeds are brought selectively and intentionally to our consciousness through the news media and other venues, including the Internet. We must make discriminating choices in regards to what we see, what we listen to, and what we feel. We must become resolute and begin to use the higher aspects of our being and consciousness in making these choices and in perceiving their effects upon us.

Right perception of what we hear and see is of extreme importance. If our perception is faulty, our thoughts, feelings, and actions will also be faulty. Right thoughts, beliefs, and actions always follow right perception. We must seek cosmic understanding of the experiences and happenings of our times. We need to become aware of and seek guidance from our spiritual self. Our spiritual eyes and ears must hear and see for us. We must request these inner faculties to see and hear as God sees and hears. There is little doubt that these need to be developed. Before we can truly see, our human eyes must become incapable of indiscriminate tears, and before we can truly hear, our human ears must lose their arbitrary sensitivity.

How do we obtain this capability? You may state that, indeed, you truly desire to see; however, you want to maintain your tears. You desire to hear and perceive correctly, but you do not wish to lose your sensitivity. With the addiction to such desires, you are proclaiming a longing to see and to hear only with your mortal, human, fallible, and transient faculties. If so, you continue to permit the small self to see for you and cause you to shed tears of illusion for what it sees. At every turn, the small self (the false self) will bring to your attention each and every detail, impressions, bits and pieces that destabilize your emotional body. This instability causes you to weep, wail, and fret, producing disharmony and imbalance of the body, mind, psychological and emotional being.

My plea is that you see with the faculties of your true self and nature—with the eyes of your higher spiritual self. Begin to hear with your inner ear and see with your

143

inner eye. The all-knowing mind within sees beyond and through all appearances and illusions. Ask the indwelling soul and Master Within to stand guard and interpret for you whatever comes into your sight and hearing. Only then is the emotional system truly protected and stimulated by the soul alone.

The divine inner faculties see with an understanding that surpasses human knowledge. Its seeing and hearing are based upon realization of its oneness with God; its non-separation from God; its remembrance of centuries and lives past; and its knowing and loving the beautiful, good, and true in the eternal now and within the human future. They are designed to reveal the truth for you. The inner, infinite faculties are within you and are for you to use.

Develop a relationship with the true self. This requires your thoughts, visualizations, realizations, contemplation, commitment, and practice. As you develop a relationship with true self, learn its attributes and use them so that you can develop a relationship with God, the source of all wisdom.

Your human faculties will become useful instruments through which cosmic wisdom and love will flow. This self is as real and functional as your physical self. However, when we depend upon our fallible human brain, eyes, and ears to give us the complete and final answers, we are accepting the product of other fallible minds. In their jobs or avocations, fallible people are occupied with programming your mind, creating, selecting, and delivering a world for you to see, hear, feel, and accept. From this subjective and limited selection of events delivered to your consciousness, you develop the idea of this limited world, and what is going on in it, as the true world. Accept this delivery and you will begin to think thoughts of the same quality as that limited world and, in so doing, you strengthen its manifestation. Be cautious of your perceptions, thoughts, beliefs, and feelings generated by the news presented for you to ingest. On a daily basis, send your creative thoughts of peace, love, harmony, and cosmic understanding into the real world, a world the masters work for and love.

How are you to become a free thinker and avoid this form of enslavement? By realizing and being aware at all times that you have choices: a choice to see and hear with the small mundane self, or to see and hear with the inner higher faculties and the Master Within. Seek to know and practice your true self.

Give birth (if I may use that analogy) to this soul expression, even though this process might seem painful and tedious to the physical self. Develop a relationship with it. Give up old patterns of thinking, believing, and speaking from the small ego self. From this inner divine birth grow cherished sons and daughters of God. This divine inner self radiates and proclaims through daily life its perfect image—the image of God.

Remember that you have complete freedom of choice. Pray affirmatively that everyone realizes this freedom of choice—realizes that God is around, through, and within you and others. With this realization, begin to practice good will and right relations in all that you do. Nothing is stronger than the spirit of humankind. The spirit of humankind shall evolve. Nothing can stop it. Pray that every heart and mind receives strength, courage, and knowledge to continue to grow in the expression of God's attributes and will. Pray that we will not grow impatient, weary, or faint. We grow stronger and develop stamina in remembering who we truly are.

We evolve as a result of all tragic experiences. Seek to understand with the inner mind and the soul's purpose. Unite others with your outpouring of love. Be determined to learn, develop, and move forward at all costs. Abolish fear and guilt, for they have no place in your life now. Replace them with knowledge that you are watched over, guided, loved, and protected. Create this security daily and always remember that cosmic law gives your thoughts the right and power to manifest and create. Create this world for you and others. You will have new values and new standards of being, a new sense of security and safety. Your capacity to love and care will constantly increase. Do not let circumstances cause you to tire or to slide back into complacency and omission. Let them serve to strengthen your resolve. Seek to manifest this expansion and extension of consciousness in your daily life.

Reject all negative thoughts as not being a part of your true nature. Send an abundance of compassion, love, peace of mind, and strength to those who are suffering. Guide the souls in transition into the light. You do not have time to feel sorry for yourself or for others. You do not have time to fear. Send that which helps; send light and love. Remember to see yourself bathed in light and love. We must become active silent workers. A host of others are with you and will join you in such endeavors.

It is the attitude and quality of the expression of human free will that creates the world in which we live, experience, and realize. God has never stopped loving humankind. Let us fight all battles by carrying the warrior within to the battlefield. With this inner warrior you fight with a spirit of love and service for the benefit of all relationships among humankind, for every nation, race, religion, and culture. God works in many ways, through many faiths, peoples, and religious agencies. Through all of these, God proclaims that there is unity and the Plan. May we seek and live that brotherhood, that unity.

We must broaden our objective from that of a personal evolution to that of the evolution of all humanity, for all living beings.

God has created laws by which the universe is governed. Humankind has continued to set these laws into creative motion through thoughts, prayers, motives, intentions, voices, and beliefs. These are the right tools. Use them always for the good. Humankind is responsible for creating the good, the beautiful, and the true, which we desire to experience. Humankind is also responsible for creating that which we do not desire to experience. We are co-creators with God. The quality of our thoughts, beliefs, and intentions will determine and manifest our world. There is work to do, and we who are on the path with knowledge of God's attributes and God's laws, and with love and goodwill in our hearts, will do that work.

It is sad to hear one say, "I am just one person; how can I make a difference?" You are not "just one person." You are inseparable from God and all fellow human beings. Your thoughts, prayers, motives, and intentions, when positive, have the potential of increasing a hundredfold, a thousandfold, for they attract constructive cosmic forces and are attracted by and drawn to the thoughts, prayers, and motives of others of like mind. These energies, by cosmic law, will seek to manifest and become experienced realities. They will express through various forms, conditions, and experiences. This has been demonstrated by an outpouring of love through individuals, groups, places, and things during times of tragedy. Look for it and you will find it. Although this outpouring of love, seen everywhere as a response to tragedy, may fade after a while, and the enthusiasm to help may seem to lessen, it is our responsibility to see that it does not. Do this with the creative power of prayers, thoughts, visualizations, beliefs, and feelings. These are the silent tools of power available to every student of mysticism. Enlightened people throughout the world also use these powerful tools. Do not grow weary or tire. Use them. Your higher self and the cosmic masters will aid you.

Love has the power to transmute hate, just as light has the power to dissipate darkness. You do not experience hate when love is flooding your mind. Unconditional love heals without going through all the lower emotions. If you are attached emotionally, permit the soul to flood you with its harmonizing love and peace.

This is a beautiful planet with beautiful, loving, and caring people. Proclaim this truth every day. Create this reality every day. Let this be your continuous and honest belief and thought. Continue saying and feeling this until sincerity kicks in and your soul joins with you. See what happens to you, to your environment, and your world. Refuse to carry the thought or belief that the world is dangerous or that God's people are evil. Your inner faculties and wisdom will tell you differently and will urge you to claim your cosmic heritage and power. Learn how to create as God creates.

All of God's creations are good. Our intention is to create that which we desire God to manifest. You are created in God's image, with God's attributes. Let your inner faculties convince you that you are one with the souls of your fellow human beings throughout the world. Your true self is not influenced by appearances of cultures, races, or religions. These are limitations, illusions, and incomplete perceptions from the material self. You are a citizen of the spiritual universe. Take full advantage of your citizenship. Appearances do not change the indwelling soul's unconditional love and sense of oneness.

At this time, Beloved, you are ready, with all humility, to sacrifice the lower self. Let it go and let the real self— God, the Master Within—be in charge of your life and all of your affairs. We have work to do! Let go of the fallible human will and invite cosmic will to express itself through you . . . as you. Let us redirect our intentions and our desires. Know that we are able to love God and others unconditionally. We are able to let God's wisdom, courage, strength, knowledge, love, light, and intelligence express themselves in, through, and about our being, and through all of our affairs and experiences. Let us elevate and expand our service to humanity. In so doing we will begin to express every attribute of God that we can express and should express in fulfilling the purpose of life—ever conforming to cosmic will and cosmic law. We will feel happy, safe, and secure in body, mind, and spirit. We will enjoy a sense of fulfillment. From this day forward let us desire this for ourselves, our fellow students on the path, our loved ones, and for all humanity.

Let's Apply What We've Learned . . .

Exercise To Promote Healing and Peace

Choose a time to perform and complete this exercise when you will not be disturbed. Read through it at least three times before performing it.

The human attributes of imagination and visualization, when properly used, can serve to regenerate our physical, emotional, mental, psychological, and spiritual nature. At this time we will use these attributes and let them lead us to purify and heal ourselves, thereby preparing us for higher cosmic service and reintegration with the One.

(If you have meditation music, you may play it at this time.)

Please sit relaxed in your seat and close your eyes. Gently ask the mind to relax your body and still your mind. Now begin to breathe slowly and deeply according to your own rhythm. Listen to the sweet vibrations of the music. Listen with the ear of the mind as if it were located in the center of your head.

With your mind, center your attention in the area of your chest and send your consciousness around the chest three times in a counterclockwise motion. Bring this motion to a stop in the front of the chest. Continue to breathe slowly and deeply, permitting your consciousness to enter into the very center of your chest. See it shining in your chest as a beautiful white light—bathing your heart and all your organs and centers within its radius. See this and feel this. Imagine and feel your lungs gently expanding and contracting as they too are bathed by the white light—a light so very full of love. The lungs bring into your body the sweet and holy air that is the divine breath of God and the breath that makes you a living soul.

Continue to breathe deeply as you permit your consciousness to flow to the area of your head, and there send it gently around the head three times in a counterclockwise motion. Slowly bring this motion to a stop, and gently let your consciousness flow to the very center of your head, and let it rest there. If you are playing music, listen to the sweet vibrations of the music. Listen with the ear of the mind as if it were located in the center of your head. Relax and let the music flow to you and bathe your being with its celestial loveliness. Continue to breathe slowly and deeply as you imagine that you are walking in nature. The sky is a beautiful shade of blue. The sun is shining so pleasantly above and gently touches your whole being.

As you walk through a beautiful meadow of green grass and colorful flowers, you approach a beautiful and gentle waterfall that descends gracefully from the top of a small mountain. As you approach the waterfall, you notice that it cascades into a small shallow circular pool before it continues flowing into a pristine stream through the meadow. As you view this scene, begin walking ceremoniously toward the waterfall and step into the shallow pool. Sense the soothing effects of the water upon your feet.

Walk further into the pool, lift your head back and walk under the gentle waterfall, permitting the pure water to bathe your face and head. Feel the wetness of the water. Sense and feel your head bathed by the refreshing stream. Feel the energies of the waters pass through your whole body, cleansing you of all impurities. Feel the refreshing water pass through your head and entire body, washing away all tensions, fears, and anxieties. See this and feel this.

As the sun shines brilliantly above, sending its rays of pure white light through the water and through your being, you are now being bathed by the cosmic water of light that purifies, refreshes, and regenerates your whole being. See and feel the lighted waters flowing through your internal organs, removing all fear, doubt, anxieties, and impurities from your mind and body, and from your emotional and psychological being.

Continue breathing slowly and deeply. As you exhale, let your inner consciousness rise within you and permit it to flow up into the heavens, shining as a beautiful and loving white light. Relax and let it flow higher and higher on its own accord, all the time shining ever more white and more bright. As your consciousness flows higher, you will notice that all your earthly worries, burdens, and fears disappear. The lighted waters of compassion have transmuted them. You are refreshed, harmonious, secure, and at peace. Relax and receive God's profound love and inner peace.

Now, in your heavenly position surrounded by God's Light and Love, realize your desire to serve humanity. You begin sending your light and love down to the earth plane. Send radiant vibrations of love, compassion, and understanding to all of humanity. You are receiving an inexhaustible cosmic source of light and love. Send both into the hearts and minds of all humankind and to all living beings—healing, blessing, strengthening, and awakening— all according to cosmic law, all according to God's will.

Perform this work for a few moments, then slowly and deliberately take five deep breaths, and as you do so, descend back to the earth plane. Feel yourself in your seat, your feet upon the floor. After your return to the earth plane, become aware of your physical surroundings. Take five more deep breaths. After the fifth breath, open your eyes, feeling refreshed and fully awake. Sit motionless with your eyes still open. Relax for a few moments, then rise and go about your regular activities.

EPILOGUE

If the Energy of Light is found within this book,

It is God stirring within you.

If Power seems to come from this book,

It is God blessing you.

If Glory shines upon this book,

It is God receiving it.

For God alone is and belongs

All Glory—All Power

So Mote It Be!

Index

Index

The Rosicrucian Order, AMORC
Purpose and Work of the Order

The Rosicrucian Order, AMORC, is a philosophical and initiatic tradition. As students progress in their studies, they are initiated into the next level or degree.

Rosicrucians are men and women around the world who study the laws of nature in order to live in harmony with them. Individuals study the Rosicrucians lessons in the privacy of their own homes on subjects such as the nature of the soul, developing intuition, classical Greek philosophy, energy centers in the body, and self-healing techniques.

The Rosicrucian tradition encourages each student to discover the wisdom, compassion, strength, and peace that already reside within each of us.

www.rosicrucian.org

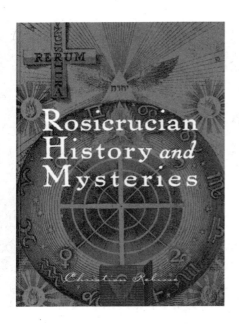

Rosicrucian History and Mysteries

by Rosicrucian author
Christian Rebisse

Softcover, 7.5 in. x 10.5 in.
244 pages

Suggested retail price: $24.95

Here is the definitive history of Rosicrucianism, from the earliest of times to the present. This book is a "must-read" for anyone interested in the Rosicrucian Order. This scholarly work is now available in English. This book is well researched—complete with endnotes, an index, a chronology, and a thematic bibliography suggesting sources for further reading. *Rosicrucian History and Mysteries* is abundantly illustrated with over 90 illustrations—many from rare and unusual sources. Your Rosicrucian library will not be complete without this exceptional volume.

For other books published by the Rosicrucian Order, AMORC, please visit www.rosicrucian.org

Treasures of the Rosicrucian Egyptian Museum

A Catalogue

by *Lisa Schwappach-Shirriff, M.A.*
Rosicrucian Egyptian Museum
Softcover, 7.5 in. x 10.5 in.
160 pages; color
Suggested retail price: $24.95

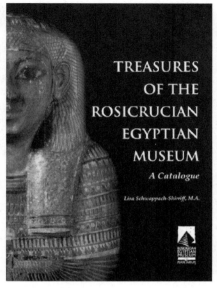

The history of the Rosicrucian Egyptian Museum in San Jose, California, began with a dream. H. Spencer Lewis, the leader of the museum's sponsoring organization, the Rosicrucian Order, AMORC, cherished this dream and through his efforts the museum came into being. Today, the Rosicrucian Egyptian Museum houses the largest collection of Egyptian, Assyrian, and Babylonian artifacts on exhibit in western North America.

This catalogue features the museum's major artifacts, including more than 250 artifact photos in color. Also included are essays providing fascinating insights into the daily life and culture of the ancient Egyptians, and a history of the Rosicrucian Egyptian Museum and its magnificent collection. With its captivating essays and beautiful photos, this museum catalogue brings ancient Egypt to life!

For other books published by the Rosicrucian Order, AMORC, please visit www.rosicrucian.org. *And for more information about the Rosicrucian Egyptian Museum, please visit* www.RosicrucianEgyptianMuseum.org